D0916994

YEADON'S REGISTER

of

L N E R

LOCOMOTIVES

Volume Nine

GRESLEY 8-COUPLED ENGINES
CLASSES O1, O2, P1, P2 & U1

ACKNOWLEDGEMENTS

Once again, my wife must have the primary tribute. Without her patience and forbearance, regular feeding and housecare, it would be quite impossible for me to continue transferring my hand-written registers into printed form for you. Hopefully, she must still consider the effort to be worthwhile, because I am given every encouragement to put my records so that fellow enthusiasts, particularly modellers, can benefit from them.

But both tables and text are only in the raw state when they leave me and it is Challenger Publications who apply the modern computer wizardry which produces such precision presentation for you. That is then complemented by the fantastic clarity with which Amadeus Press do the printing. Proof checking remains entirely my responsibility and having done it professionally for over forty years has been excellent training for achieving accuracy. I (and you) are exceedingly fortunate to have both printer and publisher fully sharing my insistence that "its near enough" has nocogeary in mechanical engineering. So I am deeply grateful to my production team, and to you for the financial support you provide.

The thousands of figures contained in each Register would inevitably destroy interest in them were they not leavened so lavishly with illustrations..For these, I am indebted to countless photographers, most of them of my own generation, and now - sadly - no longer alive. Thus many of them can see no direct credit for their help, and also a large proportion of my collection shows no indication whatever of who took the picture, or even when, and where. It is now 63 years since I began to put the LNER collection together, and I simply cannot recall the source from which many of the 30,000 were purchased, a lot of them indirectly from other collectors. So, if you see an illustration included which you are sure is a photo that you took, I would welcome you giving me the date and location via the publishers. Where possible, the photographer's name appears below the relevant plates in this volume.

First published in the United Kingdom by CHALLENGER PUBLICATIONS 1995,
This edition published by BOOKLAW/RAILBUS 2000 in association with CHALLENGER
382, Carlton Hill Nottingham NG4 1JA.
TEL: 0115 961 1066
TEL: 01422 250002
Printed and bound by The Amadeus Press, Cleckheaton, West Yorkshire.

INTRODUCTION

The five classes, totalling 96 locomotives, in this Register have one thing common to them - they were all BIG engines. Four of the classes were built for, and spent most of their lives pulling, or pushing, coal trains. The other class, although of only six engines, were special purpose express passenger engines, and prime examples of Gresley's principle, that of tailoring engines for the job that they were to do. Building dates for the five classes ranged from December 1913 to January 1943, the period when locomotive design, and railway performance reached its best years. Hopefully, this volume will pay adequate tribute to them, because now they are only memories, not one of the 96 having achieved preservation.

CLASS O1

Classes O1 and O2 (used both by the G N R and later by the L N E R) were 2-8-0 type introduced specifically for use on the main line between Peterborough and London to haul the coal traffic, loaded going south, and then the empties in the opposite direction. The boiler was common to both, so interchanges were frequent. Curiously, in 1929 Gorton works built two of these Diagram 2 boilers, which they needed for a conversation job on a couple of O4 class. One boiler remained with the O4 until it was condemned in 1943, but the other G982, from October 1934 was used by two class O1's, and one O2 before being cut up in 1945.

O1 class came into being in December 1913 to February 1914, by Doncaster building five of them, numbered 456 to 460, which for more than ten years were shedded at New England for the London coal traffic. They worked 80-wagon trains, an increase of 20 on what the Ivatt 0-8-0's were rostered to do. The 1914-18 war was probably a mixed blessing in that it delayed this class being augmented, and when circumstances did make that possible, the move to the more powerful 3-cylinder type had already begun. So class O1 was only increased by another fifteen, and by no means in orthodox fashion. Because more main line goods engines were badly needed during the war, in mid-1917, orders for boiler and frame plates, tyres and axles were placed in the United States, sufficient for ten of this class. Then in April 1918, Doncaster sent all that material to Glasgow, and gave North British Locomotive Co.an order to build the ten engines, plus another five for which they were to supply the material. Note that the order was for "engines", because the Great Northern sent 15 tenders to Glasgow, taking them from stock. Those fifteen went into service from April to October 1919, and no more were then added to the 2-cylinder variety.

Visible differences of a major kind were limited to two of that class, both concerned with feed water heating, and begun by the Great Northern. In September 1916, no.459 was fitted with an additional dome, the existing cover being extended to include it. The second dome housed trays on to which the cold feed water was pumped, before being heated to go into the boiler. It still ran so fitted, as L N E R 3459 from April 1925 until entering works in February 1927, when that boiler was taken off, and then fitted to O2 class 3461. Ex works in November 1922, no.476 carried a Worthington feed water heater and pump on its left-hand running plate, but that equipment was discarded when 3476 went in for repair in January 1927.

There were minor changes to chimney, safety valves, washout plugs, piston tail rods, lamp irons, reversing rod covers, and also to tenders, to which attention is given in the captions to the illustrations. The classification was also changed from O1 to the vacant O3 from February 1944, so that one of Thompson's standard classes could take O1.

There was also a frustrating change to their numbering, which caused confusion especially with changes of boiler in the 1946 to 1950 period. In the 1946 Thompson general renumbering, what for above twenty years had been 3456 to 3460 and 3462 to 3476 were altered to 3475 to 3494. Thus 3475/6 could apply to either the first two, or to the last two of the class. The other 18, which took 3477 to 3494 could only do so after the O2's which carried those numbers had been dealt with, and that process took from March 14th (3489 to 3934) until November 12th 1946 (3493 to 3938). So when boiler 8859 came off O2 class no.3498 in July 1946, and then started work on 3478, was that an O2 in original numbering, or was it O3 class 3459 which had been changed to 3478? Actually, that boiler went to another O2, which had begun its repair as 3478 on August 3rd, but came out of works as 3923 on August 24th 1946.

At the end of December 1946 the L N E R bought 200 W.D. 2-8-0 "Austerity" engines which they numbered 3000 to 3199, and those hastened the end for O3 class, which had by then been worked hard for 26 to 33 years. In each of the months May, June, and July 1947, one was withdrawn and cut up at Doncaster, so British Railways only acquired seventeen, of which two more were scrapped in 1948. But the other fifteen were accorded at least one more general repair, and got five-figure numbering, with only E3479 getting that interim stage, before it became 63479. Four did manage to survive into 1952, and the last one in service was 63484 which was withdrawn on December 16th 1952, all being cut up by Doncaster works. No.63488 went into works 13th February 1952 for a general repair, and conversion to oil firing, but was with drawn from running stock on the 22nd instead. After being partially dismantled, it was made Stationery Boiler 984 and served at Hunslet Power House until June 1953. It was then returned to Doncaster works and cut up there.

Livery was not the strongest feature of O1 class, their best years being 1924 to 1928. Prior to that they were in Great Northern grey with only a modicum of white lining. The LNER put them into black, with single red lining, 471 with L & N E R being the first in April 1923. The next three, 457 in August, 463 in October, and 460 in December all got the Area suffix N, but the other 16, from 3458 in February 1924 to 3469 in April 1925 got that LNER numbering along with their red lined black paint. After the June 1928 painting economies became effective, O1 class were just unlined black through to withdrawal. From July 1942 only N E was used, but all except 3487/92 did have L N E R restored in 1946/47. After nationalisation, 63476/9/80/1/3-6/8/91/3 got that numbering, and only 63476 failed to get plate on smokebox door. Seven of them 63475/6/8/9/82/4/8 survived to get the smaller size of the B.R. emblem - when you could see it for the black smoke, coal dust, and almost complete neglect by cleaners. But they must have been very handsome revenue earners for Great Northern, LNER and British Railways.

Used entirely for moving minerals (almost wholly coal, and iron ore, but also bricks), there was no opportunity to be

The initial five engines nos.456 to 460 were built at Doncaster from December 1913 to February 1914, and originally their boiler was fed by a Weir pump, but those had been removed by the Great Northern, because normal injectors had been proved to be adequate. No.459 is in the grey paint used for this class.

hauled by one of them, nor were they brake fitted for working a passenger train. Between April 2nd 1939 and September 24th 1942 I did however record all except one of them, and on the ex-GN main line between Doncaster and Holloway. The last one no.3470, eluded me until September 4th 1945 when I saw it on shed at York, where it had worked in on one of the iron ore trains from High Dyke (just south of Grantham where it was then shedded) with a load to be taken on to Tees-side furnaces.

CLASS O2

The first order for O1 class was for five engines and six boilers, of which the five put on the engines were fitted with the Doncaster type superheater, but the spare had one of Robinson type, and was not completed until July 1917. By then, Gresley had developed his first 3-cylinder design using his patented conjugated valve gear, and so the extra boiler started work in May 1918 on engine no.461. That engine was given class 02 on the GNR, which it retained in the LNER classification effective from the end of 1923, and had a 6% greater tractive effort than the preceding O1 class. The three smaller diameter cylinders had lighter pistons which reduced wear in the cylinders, and their effect was more evenly spread across the engine.

Experience with no.461 led to improvements being made to the steam flow, and also to a lighter form of 2 to 1 levers in the middle valve gear. That revised arrangement was first used in 1920 on the big 2-6-0 type which later became LNER class K3, and then also in the next ten O2 class engines ordered from the North British Locomotive Co. which were numbered 477 to 486 and built in 1921. No.461 remained the sole example of its valve gear arrangement, and the LNER classed it simply as O2, but

gave Part 1 to the ten built in 1921, which were also to the GNR generous load gauge, and had half-inch larger diameter cylinders than no.461. On 26th February 1923, Doncaster works were given an order for ten more of the class, to which another five were added a month later, nos 487 to 501 being allocated to them. All except two of those numbers were already available, so the two old saddle tank engines carrying 494 and 496 were transferred to the Duplicate List to free them for the O2's. Despite thirteen of these 2-8-0's working their first twenty years from New England shed on the London coal traffic, the L N E R must have initially envisaged that they might be used on other sections where the load gauge was more restrictive than on the GN main line. All fifteen were built to a maximum height of 13' 1" instead of the 13' 4" of their predecessors, and were to the Composite Load Gauge which the LNER had established. To do so, the cab roof was lower, with the whistle in front of the cab instead of on top of it, and a chimney of reduced height was fitted; they were given Part 2 of the class. The two not at first sent to New England shed were 3496 which worked ten months from Doncaster shed before joining the others, whilst 3501 initially worked for nine months in the North Eastern Area from Newport shed, and for neither of those two allocations was there any need to be of reduced height.

By 1932 the G.E. line was capable of taking bigger and heavier engines, and the new hump shunting yard at Whitemoor (March) had become effective, making possible more efficient handling of the London coal traffic via that route, which was also quite considerable. For use on it, another sixteen class O2 were built by Doncaster, eight numbered 2954 to 2961 in 1932, four numbered 2430 to 2433 in 1933, and for those twelve, tenders were taken from Scottish J38 class engines which did not need either 4200 gallons capacity or water pick-up gear. As an early

GNR 461 which Doncaster completed in May 1919 was a development of the O1 class. There were now three cylinders, and derived valve gear for the middle one, laying down the principle which Gresley then followed and made standard. It was, and remained, a singleton, its inclined outside cylinders clearly differentiating it from all the later engines of the class. *G.W.Goslin.*

Group Standard type, they had stepped top to their side panels so by 1932/33 were readily recognisable as second-hand. The order was completed in 1934 with nos 2434 to 2437, and for those four, Doncaster built new 4200 gallon tenders with flush sides. The use of 2430 to 2437 was a case of history repeating itself, because the first LNER engines with those numbers had been built in 1889 for the Hull & Barnsley Railway simply for hauling coal from pits in the West Riding to Alexandra Dock in Hull to be exported.

The sixteen numbered 2954 to 2961 and 2430 to 2437 were all allocated to March shed to work the G.E. coal traffic to London, and had a maximum height of 13' 0", achieved by slightly cutting down the dome cover, but they were also provided with a much more congenial cab having side windows, whilst their Group Standard tender gave enhanced coal and water capacity. Those differences were marked by putting them into Part 3 of O2 class.

Finally, greatly increased traffic due to the 1939 war led to a further 25 being built of the Part 3 type, ten ordered by Gresley on 3rd June 1940, and fifteen by Thompson on 9th June 1941, less than five weeks after Gresley's sudden and unexpected death. Numbers 3833 to 3857 were given to them, 22 going into traffic in 1942, and the final three in January 1943. Tenders for them were found by depriving D49 class passenger engines which no longer had need of Group Standard type, thus saving 634 tons of steel for diversion into munitions of war. So class O2 ultimately totalled 67, of which in 1943/44, five were rebuilt with Diagram 100A boiler, and which then became Part 4 of the class.

Although no fundamental alteration was made, changes were many and varied, and are described comprehensively in Part 6B of the R.C.T.S. series of volumes on Locomotives of the LNER for which I was one of the main panel of authors. But the illustrations included in this Register endeavour to portray all those of significance to modellers concerned to get the precise appearance of whichever member of the class they select to build.

My first recording was of 2954 at Stratford shed on 4th April 1936, followed by 3477 on an up goods at Abbots Ripton on 7th May 1937. By 1946, when they were re-numbered 3921 to 3987 in order of building sequence, I had logged all except five, and of those, 3956/71/3/81 were seen in 1947 still as LNER. Completion of this class eluded me until 25th April 1950 when I saw British Railways no.63970 taking a coal train to Whitemoor through Lincoln. A few sightings were well off their normal track, viz.3483 on 22nd September 1944 on a down goods at Bulwell; 3486 (a Part 4) on 29th May 1944 in Tyne Dock shed; 3835 on 19th May 1943 outside Dairycoates shed in Hull, and 3849 on 6th February 1943 with a goods at Trafford Park.

By doubly good fortune, I was actually hauled (albeit briefly) by 63933 on 29th August 1950 when I was returning from London to Hull in the Yorkshire Pullman. 60067 LADAS was doing about 70 m.p.h. down the 1 in 200 towards Holme when its left hand side connecting rod snapped. Very luckily it broke in the middle of its length, and the end that was flailing round, cut into but did not dig in to the sleepers, otherwise LADAS would have been thrown on to its side, with consequent unpredictable damage to the train. Driver Howard of King's Cross shed brought the train safely to a stop in three-quarters of a mile, at Holme station, but told the Press that the way the engine had bumped and bounced made him sure it was off the rails. Quite soon, O2 class 63933 detached from a following goods train, came on to the rear of the Pullman and drew us back to a cross-over from down to up line. Then V2 class 60908 arrived from Peterborough to haul us to Doncaster, and as we approached the

3

The first of the two engines, no.2393 was completed on 27th June 1925, just in time to run as Item 12 in the Stockton & Darlington Railway Centenary Procession. It then began work at the end of July from New England shed on the mineral trains to London, and remained so occupied for the rest of its life of exactly 20 years.

stricken Pacific, we could see the severe damage to the sleepers on the down line. Even so, I was only 95 minutes late into Hull, and with unique haulage by an O2 to my credit. Only when I read in the next morning's *Yorkshire Post* did I realise how very nearly I might NOT have been unable to do so.

During the 1950's many O2's were seen in Hull on oil tank trains from the refinery at Saltend, but in 1963 when the final forty were withdrawn, we were spared the sad sight of Hull's Albert Draper breaking up even a single O2 amongst the 732 to which his gang applied the torch. For a purely mineral engine, O2's design was about the most elegant.

CLASS P1

This was a case of Gresley saying "Anything you can do, I can do better". Just as the 60 wagon London coal trains hauled by Ivatt's Q1 class were up-staged by Gresley's O1 class in lifting the load to 80 wagons, so a design based on his Pacifics provided him with further scope. On 18th August 1924, Doncaster were given an order to build "Two 3-cylinder 2-8-2 Mikado 5' 2" Coal Engines with Booster", to be numbered 2393 and 2394. Ex works on 27th June 1925, no.2393 was just in time to be included a week later in the Stockton & Darlington Centenary Procession, whilst when 2394 followed on 14th November, it was seen to have not one, but two Gresley snifting valves abaft its chimney. That indicated something different, and we soon learned that whereas 2393 had the usual 32-element Robinson superheater, on 2394 was an M.L.S. 'E double' type superheater, which had some 62 elements.

The appearance of the two P1's was already familiar because much of it was based on Gresley's Pacifics, so the 'look-alike' 2-8-2 was sure of a favourable reception. That close relationship was emphasised when 2393 had its first boiler change, its original being put on ST SIMON and its replacement came from FLYING FOX, so would have steamed successfully on the latter's 392-mile non-stop 'Flying Scotsman' runs.

After 2394's special superheater was changed to the customary 32-element Robinson type in November 1931, its original boiler did a further turn of duty in 2394, but in July 1934 was replaced by one taken from SCEPTRE. In November 1942 no.2394, followed in January 1943 by 2393, were changed to boilers working at 220 instead of 180 lb per sq.in. As was the case in their first six years when the Gresley snifter difference clearly identified which was which, during their final three years the shape of the dome cover enabled that to be done again. On the higher pressure boilers 2394's had the 'banjo' type steam collector, but 2393 had one with the normal circular type. To our gratification, Arthur Cook took photos of both whilst they were waiting to be cut up at Doncaster works, their rarity far outweighing the handicap of the wartime paper negatives he was compelled to use. He has kindly allowed me to include that differential evidence in this Register.

The original intention was for them to work 100 wagon coal trains which meant their being capable of hauling 1600 ton loads, and to assist getting such a heavy load on the move, both were fitted with a 2-cylinder auxiliary engine under the cab which powered the carrying wheels. Appropriately referred to as a 'booster', it proved to be more troublesome then effective, because its purpose was found to be more easily achieved by changing the driving technique to full open regulator and changing the cut-off. Despite extensive trials, and persistent effort spread over ten years usage, in 1937 both boosters were taken out of use, to the regret only of the fitting staff at New England shed, who were then deprived of prolific overtime pay on repairs to the booster equipment. As on the Pacifics there were some similar changes of detail, and these are covered by the illustrations I have included. The tenders were a one-off design peculiar to these two engines, and after the engines were withdrawn in July 1945, their tenders 5293 and 5294 were sent to Darlington works on 29th August 1945, where after some modification, they served another 13 years with rebuilds from B17 to B2 class.

After my move to Hull in 1932 changed me from an LNWR to an LNER observer, I recorded seeing 2393 outside Doncaster works on 7th May 1934 awaiting a trial trip from a general repair. 2394 was seen doing what it was built for on 2nd May 1940 at Holme, working a down train of empty coal wagons, returning them from London to Peterborough.

Understandably, there was no chance of ever being hauled by this class, but there were three opportunities of getting closely acquainted with them. No.2393 was on display in the July 1925 celebrations at Darlington to mark the S & D Centenary, and on 5/6th June 1937 it was featured in a rolling stock exhibition at New Barnet. No. 2394 was included in a similar event at Cambridge on 7th and 8th May 1938, but opportunities to see either away from the former G N main line were otherwise practically non-existent.

CLASS P2

This class was Gresleys' Enigma Variations - six to the same theme, but all of them different. However, they did have one constant feature in that they kept the name and number with which they first appeared throughout their time in P2 class.
2001 COCK O' THE NORTH had rotary cam operated poppet valves.
2002 EARL MARISCHAL had two pairs of smoke deflectors.
2003 LORD PRESIDENT the first with Bugatti type front end.
2004 MONS MEG had by-pass controlled blastpipe.
2005 THANE OF FIFE had only a single blastpipe and chimney.
2006 WOLF OF BADENOCH had longer firebox with a combustion chamber.

To pronounce on their performance also poses an enigma. They were designed and built for eliminating the need to use two engines and crews on the restaurant car, and sleeping car trains running between Edinburgh (Waverley), Dundee, and Aberdeen. On that score they were supremely successful. To get the power required, and to ensure the adhesion to apply it, Gresley had to stretch the design of an express passenger locomotive further than had been considered the practical limit in this country. To get the required power involved a grate area of no less than 50 sq.feet, and also four pairs of coupled wheels had to be of adequate diameter, 6' 2" being the desirable minimum. That gave a rigid wheelbase of 37' 11" against 35' 9" on the Pacifics they were to supersede, and resulted in a 2-wheel pony truck having to be used for guidance at the front instead of the increased length of a 4-wheel bogie. Lack of a bogie, combined with that lengthy coupled wheelbase were to cause real difficulties on the 131 miles between Edinburgh and Aberdeen, because they were almost wholly a succession of sinuous curves. From my own travels over it (which were quite frequent in the 1940's and 1950's) I seem to recall that the only straight sections of significant length were the 1Z\x miles across the Forth, and the 2 miles across the Tay Bridges. Soon after they went into service there, it was found that the pony truck did not provide enough guidance, and that the leading coupled wheels were having to help when the engine was entering a curve, which had a drastic effect on the crank pins of the coupling rods. As had been found on the Pacifics, the middle big end proved troublesome, and doubtless aggravated by the curvature problem, at least three known cases of crank axle breakage are known to have occurred. Changing the pony truck from swing link to side spring control could well have minimised the guidance trouble, and indeed the Chief Draughtsman at Doncaster, Teddy Windle, did his best to have that adopted. But executive power had changed to Thompson,

On 4th March 1933 an order was placed on Doncaster works for "2 Tender Engines of 2-8-2 type to be classed P2, for Scottish Area", and the first one was allocated the number 2981. On 13th April the order was reduced to a single engine and the number for it was changed to 2001. Here is how it was turned out by Doncaster on 22nd May 1934 fitted with rotary cam operated valve gear, and with straight nameplates. *British Railways.*

and he would not sanction it, being more concerned with eliminating Gresley Mikados and making them into his idea of a Thompson Pacific.

It has never been revealed how, at a time when the war situation was so desperate, he was allowed to get away with wasting steel, and also precious labour, only to ruin powerful engines, and turn them into a hideous looking design, of questionable worth. Wartime train loadings of 600 to 800 tons on the passenger trains out of King's Cross simply cried out for the six P2's to be transferred to deal with them, and on the GN main line, even as far as York there were no curves severe enough to bother them. Thompson could have saved the LNER a lot of money, and avoided loss of face, and friends, for himself, if he had co-operated with the operating people in making that transfer. No wonder that a knighthood never came his way.

So between January 1943 and December 1944, P2 class perished and disappeared; it only remains to record what I knew of it. 2001 was less than 4 months old when I saw it on 16th September 1934 at Doncaster works in course of a light repair, and 2002 was no more than 10 days old when I was in its cab whilst it had paused at York to participate in an exhibition of engines and rolling stock whilst on its delivery journey to Scottish Area. Of the four built in June to September 1936, by July 1938 I had seen 2003/5/6 but 2004 eluded completion until 18th July 1941. Curiously, that was the only one that I managed to be hauled by - on 24th July 1942 in the 7.55 p.m. from Glasgow (Queen Street) to Edinburgh (Waverley). I think its driver's name must have been Nelson, because he sure turned a blind eye to any requirement for the rear end of his train to be banked up the Cowlairs incline. The next time I was accelerated so swiftly was when my wife and I left Yeadon (Leeds-Bradford) airport in a Boeing 747 Jumbo on a direct flight to Toronto.

It might be of interest to mention the trains on which I recorded all six P2 class: 2001 18th July 1941 leaving Edinburgh (Waverley) with the 9.55 a.m. to Aberdeen: 2002 20th July 1942 arriving in Waverley with the 12.40 p.m. from Aberdeen: 2003 18th July 1938 at Kinghorn working the 8.40 a.m. slow Dundee to Edinburgh: 2004 18th July 1941 in Waverley on the 9.42 a.m.

arrival from Aberdeen: 2005 18th July 1938 on the 10.20 a.m. from Aberdeen arriving in Dundee: 2006 7th October 1937, solo in York, going to Doncaster for a light repair.

Deliberately, I have avoided reference to too much technical detail, because as a main editor of the R.C.T.S. Locomotives of the LNER, I helped to research and write the very comprehensive account of the class which appears in Part 6B of that work. So in this Volume of my Register I have concentrated on including photographs of all significant visible changes of detail in order to be of maximum assistance to model makers.

CLASS U1

This was the longest, heaviest, and most powerful engine ever to run on British railway lines, not surprisingly, because really it was two welded into one, contradicting our elementary school arithmetic that 'two into one would NOT go'. Practically the whole of this engine's life was also spent pushing trains, instead of pulling them, and the times when it hauled one could be counted on one hand. In the Doncaster Works Engine Order Book the relevant entry is for "2-8-0 - 0-8-2 Garratt Tank Engine, built by Beyer, Peacock & Co. Manchester", with figure 2 (later altered to 1) and allocated numbers 2395 and (in pencil) 2396. Intriguingly in the Boiler Order section of that book there is a firm entry for 7963 & 7964 allocated to 2 Garratt boilers, although the figure 2 has been altered - in pencil - to 1. Second thoughts must also have applied to its allocation, because of the entry against it "To be included in the G N Section stock - see C.M.E. 1347/2 of 24.7.25". Strangely, all its LNER work was done on the G.C. Section, its first shed being Barnsley, but after only two months being transferred to Mexborough. A second Garratt was never ordered, and reference to it in official papers ceased in March 1925.

The movement of coal from pits in South Yorkshire to power generating stations in Lancashire and Cheshire provided a regular traffic of almost a train an hour, day and night, throughout normal working days. Averaging about 60 wagons they were assembled in the Wath concentration yard, giving a load of about 1000 tons

to be hauled. They were then worked west along the seven mile, goods only, branch through Worsborough, south of Barnsley to reach the Barnsley-Penistone line at West Silkstone Junction. The last 3^1/$_2$ miles to that junction were up a formidable gradient of 1 in 40, and the sole justification for this Garratt was for it to push coal trains up that slope. In the brief intervals when it was not so engaged, it was at the bottom of the bank, at Wentworth Junction in a siding where coal and water facilities for it were provided, and the three sets of crews who worked it changed over there as required. So, nominally allocated to Mexborough shed, it left there early on a Monday morning, and did not return until in the afternoon of the following Saturday, for weekend servicing. Between those times it simply worked its hardest up the hill, and then drifted light down the 3^1/$_2$ mile incline. To see that Garratt at work, or even at all during the week, needed planned and pertinacious effort, because the location was very much off the beaten track. It was so remote that in recent years a criminal blackmailer thought it was safe enough to have his money dropped from an overbridge there, fully confident of recovering it later when clear to do so. By sheer chance, a man out walking his dog got there first, which led to justice being duly done.

I never reached that area, but on 29th October 1934 I first saw 2395 in Doncaster works yard whilst it was there for a heavy repair. Subsequently on three Sunday visits to its shed I was able to assess its size at close quarters. On none of those occasions was I told that "I could have it, if I could pull it". That only came out when I saw its United States equivalent 'Big Boy' in preservation at Bellows Falls in 1978.

(above) **No. 2395 built by Beyer, Peacock & Co. Manchester in June 1925, and delivered to Gorton on Sunday 21st June. Here, on the 23rd, it was working to Doncaster to be prepared for participating in a Centenary exhibition. Note that, as delivered by the makers, its buffers had circular heads and flanges, and there were no lamp irons fitted on top of the buffer beam. It was still painted only in shop grey, but had LNER displayed both fore and aft.**

(below) **This official photograph was taken on 7th August 1925. Following further trials 2395 was first allocated to Barnsley shed as from 21st August, but two months later it was moved to Mexborough for its shed maintenance.** *L.N.E.R.*

There was one occasion when it might have been possible for me to have a ride behind it, but I had not become a Rotarian soon enough. On Monday 31st March 1930 the Rotary Club of Sheffield arranged with the LNER for a train of 20 special purpose wagons to be shown to Sheffield industrialists who could be potential users of them. The wagons ranged from a 150 ton cantilever set and a 70 ton transformer set, through Belgian and German train ferry wagons, to an insulated meat container and a 10 ton steam heated banana van. The Sheffield Chamber of Commerce were also involved in the event, and as their then President was Mr (later Sir) Ronald Matthews, no wonder the LNER made such a big production of it. You will be wondering what this has to do with the Garratt. The wagons were assembled in Hexthorpe sidings at Doncaster where the Press were given copious information about them, and access for photography. Then it was no.2395 which hauled them to Sheffield (Victoria) station, its only known LNER occasion when it pulled instead of pushed a train. Shortly before arriving, (probably at Attercliffe Road), the train halted for the Lord Mayor of Sheffield to join the crew on the footplate. The wagons were then put on display at Victoria, there was luncheon in the adjoining Hotel, which was earned by listening to the Assistant Goods Manager speaking on the subject of "The Railway and the Trader".

Completely out of its normal environment, on 11/12th May 1935, no.2395 was a surprise inclusion in an exhibition of locomotives and rolling stock held in Hunslet (Leeds) goods yard, presumably as a foil to 10000 the 'Hush-Hush' and 2750 PAPYRUS which only two months before had done a fully authenticated 108 mph, or it could have been to contrast its 87' 3" length against fellow exhibit Y3 class Sentinel shunter no.96 at 18' 10Z\v"; in short, a difference almost of the same overall length of a Gresley Pacific with corridor tender.

After its centre-stage appearance at Leeds, 2395 resumed pushing coal trains up the Worsborough bank for a further nineteen years, serving a valuable but hum-drum purpose. By 1949 work had been able to re-start on the electrification of the Manchester-Sheffield line via Woodhead (which the six years of war had interrupted) and that included the Worsborough branch. By now changed from no.2395 to no.9999, the Garratt's boiler was 24 years old and rapidly nearing its sell-by date, and there was no spare for it. Soon the engine would be redundant in South Yorkshire, and before the expense of a new boiler could be justified, especially in a climate where accountants were gaining ascendancy over those who had to operate the railways, a new venue for useful work by the Garratt had to be found. Someone had the idea that it could replace the 0-10-0 "Big Bertha" at pushing passenger trains up the Lickey incline south of Birmingham, that engine being even older by 5Z\x years. On 7th March 1949 the Garratt (now 69999) was transferred from Mexborough to Bromsgrove, where the London Midland men found it to be very different from their no.2290 and they made a poor job of operating it. Here was yet another example of men deciding that another line's engine was "no good" compared with what they had been used to for years. So they did not make the effort to work it properly, and managed to have it returned to Mexborough in November 1950. One of their gripes was the hard physical work young firemen had to put in to feed a 56Z\x sq.ft grate, so money was spent on converting it to oil fuel firing by Gorton works in August to December 1952. Various difficulties at getting it effective and efficient arose, leading to assorted modifications having to be tried. It then did three test runs as far as Crowden, actually hauling goods wagons making up about a 600 ton load, spread over the October 1953 to March 1954 period. Neither enthusiasm nor determination for putting it right seem to have been forthcoming, but it was much too big to hide or ignore. At the end of June 1955 it was again sent to work on the Lickey incline, but even without the prodigious amounts of coal to shovel, it was no more favourably received than on its previous visit. One of the drivers must have been a member of Greenpeace, or of Friends of the Earth because he discovered that when he shut off steam at the top of the bank, he could send a cloud of dense black, oily smoke across the adjacent golf course. Golf is serious business to influential businessmen, and such uncouth interference was intolerable. By 13th September, that had filtered through various channels until it had reached someone with the ability to say enough was enough, and forthwith 69999 ceased work on the Lickey and was put into store, first at Burton-on-Trent, from where on 3rd October it was sent, via Chesterfield and Chinley (not via Woodhead) to Gorton, also for storage. Withdrawal from stock was made on 23rd December 1955, when its journey to Doncaster works for cutting up took its official total mileage to 425,213.

Whatever one's LNER loyalties, it seems inappropriate to conclude with "sic transit gloria" for the Garratt. Sales of my Registers however have enabled me to commission the building of a finely detailed OO gauge model of 2395, motored at both ends. I made the stipulation that both sets of driving wheels should be set to revolve in the SAME direction, unlike some Crewe uncoupled compounds are reported to have been prone to do occasionally.

L.N.E.R.

2–8–8–2 "GARRATT" BANKING ENGINE. TYPE U.1.

GAUGE OF TRACK	CYLINDERS				DRIVING WHEEL DIAMETER	BOILER		FIREBOX		TUBES.		
	FORE UNIT (3)		REAR UNIT (3)			Inside Dia.	Pressure.	Length outside	Width outside	Number	Diam.	Length between Tube Plates.
	Diam.	Stroke	Diam.	Stroke								
4 ft. 8½ in.	18½ in.	26 in.	18½ in.	26 in.	4 ft. 8 in.	6ft. $10\frac{7}{16}$ in.	180 lbs.	9 ft. 5 in.	7 ft. 6¼ in.	259 45	2 in. 5¼ in.	13 ft. 5 in.

WHEEL BASE					WEIGHT IN WORKING ORDER						
FORE UNIT		REAR UNIT		Total	FORE UNIT			REAR UNIT			Total
Driving	Unit	Driving	Unit		Bogie	Coupled	Unit	Bogie	Coupled	Unit	
17 ft. 10½ in.	26 ft. 6½ in.	17 ft. 10½ in.	26 ft. 6½ in.	79 ft. 1 in.	17 tons 4 c.	71 tons 0 c.	88 tons 4 c.	16 tons 9 c.	72 tons 18 c.	89 tons 17 c.	178 tons 1c.

FUEL	EVAPORATING SURFACES—SQUARE FT.				SUPER-HEATING SURFACE sq. ft.	GRATE		TRACTIVE POWER AT 85% Boiler Pressure	FACTOR OF ADHESION
Kind	Tubes	Flues	Firebox	Total		Length	Width		
						$101\frac{9}{16}$ ins.	80⅛ ins.		
Coal	1819·5	825	223·5	2868	650	Area 56·5 sq. ft.		72940 lbs.	4·4

CAPACITY: WATER. 5000 GALS. {FORE UNIT—2800 GALS. / REAR UNIT—2200 GALS.} COAL. 7 TONS.

CASTING THE CYLINDERS

The whole purpose of any locomotive is to move loads, whether they be of wagons containing goods, or of coaches carrying passengers. The ability of steam engines to do so lies primarily in their cylinders, the manufacture of which is a complex, and very skilled operation. It begins with designers and draughtsmen having exercised their imagination, and then put clear instruction on to drawings, from which expert workers in wood make the patterns, the assembly of which results in a sculpture worthy of Henry Moore, but far more useful, and even attractive than most of his output. The completed pattern then forms the heart of a moulding box into which sand has to be accurately shaped, and consolidated so that it can cope with the weight and heat of three to four tons of molten iron, poured into the box from a ladle. Every particle of air in the mould has to be completely replaced by iron in liquid state, and the resultant casting must be devoid of the slightest blowhole. After cooling, the box can be opened and the sand broken away, to leave a very heavy and rough casting which is then fettled, and passed to the skilled machinists, who transform it to precise dimensions, which was expressed in the order of thousands of an inch. One of my friends, a fellow Rotarian always claimed that 'engineering had never been the same since thous were invented'. Then the erectors take over and finish the job.

The 3-cylinder casting could truly be regarded both as a work of art, and as a triumph of scientific skill. Its genesis, gestation, and the ability of those responsible for producing its completion commanded scant notice from those of us who are locomotive enthusiasts and observers, so the eight photographs which follow are a tribute to those unseen, and unsung, railwaymen. They do not represent a connected series of the same casting, but they do show the main stages of the process, and all are concerned with engines dealt with in this volume. Those who now interfere with work in the sacred name of Health and Safety will gnash their teeth at the photographs which show molten metal being poured. Just look at the flimsy stance of the man propped up on a wheelbarrow, and the complete absence of goggles, gloves, helmets, and protective footwear, and yet they were proud of producing Cock o' the North out of those conditions; the picture shows nothing of the heat, dust, and fumes in which they worked.

I am grateful for the help and advice of Brian Smith Esq. the Managing Director of Hull's leading ironfounders, for the technicalities described above and in the photograph captions, which the LNER's Doncaster official photographer provided some 25 years ago.

(right) **Wood pattern for casting of cylinder block used by the 8-coupled engines. Note that no core boxes are shown.**

(below) **Bottom (or Drag) portion of the three-part moulding box.**

(above) **Bottom mould, showing cylinder cores in place.**   *(below)* **About 3 or 4 tons of molten cast iron being poured.**

(above) **Rod feeding of heavy sections to ensure a sound casting.**   *(below)* **Rough casting after knock out from moulding box.**

(above) **Fettled (i.e. cleaned) casting ready for machining.**

(below) **A finished casting, ready for erection on the frame of an 8-coupled engine.**

CLASS O1

3456

Doncaster 1411.

To traffic 12/1913.

REPAIRS:
Don. 5/4-19/8/22.**G.**
Don. 27/8-12/12/24.**G.**
Don. 25/1-26/4/26.**L.**
Don. 6/7-24/9/27.**G.**
Don. 15/2-24/3/28.**L.**
Don. 7/12/29-11/2/30.**G.**
Gor. 22/7-5/11/32.**G.**
Gor. 22/11/34-26/1/35.**G.**
Don. 26/11/35-8/1/36.**G.**
Don. 6/2-14/3/38.**G.**
Don. 1/2-8/4/40.**G.**
Don. 22/3-23/5/42.**G.**
Don. 29/5-14/8/43.**L.**
Don. 13-29/9/43.**L.** *After Collision.*
Don. 9/3-21/4/45.**G.**
Don. 19/9-19/10/46.**L.**
Don. 27/2-25/5/47.**G.**
Don. 18/9-4/1/49.**G.**

BOILERS:
7234.
7239 *(ex3461)* 24/9/27.
7690 *(ex3489)* 5/11/32.
7713 *(ex3499)* 26/1/35.
7718 *(ex3475)* 14/3/38.
8463 *(ex3462)* 23/5/42.
9396 *(ex3984)* 25/5/47.
4404 *(ex3479)* 4/11/49.

SHEDS:
New England.
Hornsey 23/6/30.
New England 26/2/31.
Mexborough 31/5/37.
Doncaster 4/1/38.
Frodingham 7/4/46.
Doncaster 17/1/48.
Retford 27/8/50.

RENUMBERED:
3475 22/12/46.
63475 4/11/49.

CONDEMNED:
24/7/51.
Cut up at Doncaster.

3457

Doncaster 1412.

To traffic 12/1913.

REPAIRS:
Don. 24/6-3/7/20.**L.**
Don. 25/4-25/8/23.**G.**
Don. 1/2-10/4/26.**G.**
Don. 18/5-10/8/28.**G.**
Don. 27/4-1/6/29.**G.**
Don. 11/7-29/8/31.**G.**
Gor. 6/1-3/2/34.**G.**
Don. 1-29/2/36.**G.**
Don. 23/4-14/5/38.**G.**
Don. 17/2-9/3/40.**G.**
Don. 13/6-25/7/42.**G.**
Don. 13/5-17/6/44.**G.**
Don. 6/4-4/5/46.**G.**
Don. 24/2-27/3/48.**G.**
Don. 3/7-26/8/50.**G.**

BOILERS:
7235.
7519 *(ex3470)* 10/4/26.
7512 *(ex3468)* 3/2/34.
8857 *(new)* 29/2/36.
7502 *(ex3465)* 14/5/38.
9362 *(new)* 25/7/42.
9247 *(ex3489)* 4/5/46.
21000 *(ex3963)* 8/50.

SHEDS:
New England.
Mexborough 31/5/37.
Doncaster 18/1/38.
Grantham 6/5/45.
Doncaster 25/6/45.
Frodingham 4/5/46.
Doncaster 18/1/48.
Retford 25/2/51.

RENUMBERED:
3476 10/11/46.
63476 27/3/48.

CONDEMNED:
17/3/52.
Cut up at Doncaster.

3458

Doncaster 1413.

To traffic 1/1914.

REPAIRS:
Don. 6/4-23/7/21.**G.**
Don. 12/10/23-11/2/24.**G.** *As 3458.*
Don. 11/6-10/10/25.**G.**
Don. 22/7-25/11/27.**G.**
Don. 23/4-18/7/30.**G.**
Gor. 17/11/32-4/3/33.**G.**
Don. 27/5-29/7/35.**G.**
Don. 14/3-20/5/37.**G.**
Don. 12/6-26/8/39.**G.**
Don. 23/3-30/4/41.**G.**
Don. 9/12/42-3/2/43.**G.**
Don. 26/5-10/6/44.**G.**
Don. 12/5-15/6/45.**G.**
Don. 17/3-25/4/46.**L.**
Don. 7/2-4/5/47.**G.**
Don. 14/6-15/7/48.**L.**
Don. 18/7-26/8/49.**G.**

BOILERS:
7236.
7521 *(ex3472)* 25/11/27.
7689 *(ex3486)* 4/3/33.
9161 *(new)* 26/8/39.
4405 *(ex3487)* 15/6/45.
8856 *(ex3936)* 26/8/49.

SHEDS:
New England.
Doncaster 26/8/39.
Frodingham 25/4/46.
Doncaster 17/1/48.
Retford 18/3/51.

RENUMBERED:
3477 27/10/46.
63477 15/7/48.

CONDEMNED:
8/10/51.
Cut up at Doncaster.

3459

Doncaster 1415.

To traffic 1/1914.

REPAIRS:
Don. 23/2-23/9/22.**G.**
Don. 30/10/24-11/4/25.**G.**

Don. 21/2-4/6/27.**G.**
Don. 12/3-18/7/28.**G.**
Don. 2/8-16/10/30.**G.**
Gor. 8/2-13/5/32.**G.**
Gor. 12/2-27/3/34.**L.**
Don. 6/6-13/7/35.**G.**
Don. 5/3-26/5/37.**G.**
Don. 19/11-31/12/37.**G.**
Don. 28/7-7/10/39.**G.**
Don. 6/6-23/7/41.**G.**
Don. 7/3-13/4/42.**L.**
Don. 28/4-15/6/43.**L.**
Don. 12/5-16/6/45.**G.**
Don. 29/12/46-8/3/47.**G.**
Don. 23/4-1/6/48.**G.**
Don. 4-13/8/48.**L.**
Don. 7/3-24/4/50.**G.**

BOILERS:
7237.
7238 *(ex3460)* 4/6/27.
7505 *(ex3474)* 13/5/32.
9163 *(new)* 7/10/39.
9390 *(ex3978)* 8/3/47.
9471 *(ex3940)* 1/6/48.
9396 *(ex3475)* 24/4/50.

SHEDS:
New England.
Colwick 27/11/25.
New England 19/8/35.
Doncaster 7/10/39.
Frodingham 7/4/46.
Doncaster 18/1/48.
Retford 3/12/50.

RENUMBERED:
3478 5/11/46.
63478 1/6/48.

CONDEMNED:
15/10/51.
Cut up at Doncaster.

3460

Doncaster 1418.

To traffic 2/1914.

REPAIRS:
Don. 18/7-21/9/22.**L.**
Don. 10/8-22/12/23.**G.** *As 460N.*
Don. 4/1-30/3/26.**G.**

WORKS CODES:- Cow - Cowlairs. Dar - Darlington. Don - Doncaster. Ghd - Gateshead. Gor - Gorton. Inv - Inverurie. Str - Stratford.

REPAIR CODES:- **C/H** - Casual Heavy. **C/L** - Casual Light. **G** - General. **H** - Heavy. **H/I** - Heavy Intermediate. **L** - Light. **L/I** - Light Intermediate. **N/C** - Non-Classified.

13

No.474 was the final engine of the fifteen built by North British Locomotive Co. at their Atlas Works, all having a second-hand tender supplied by Doncaster. Note the maker's plate mounted on the side of the smokebox, instead of the Doncaster position at the front end of the frame.

Don. 12/11/27-19/1/28.**G.**
Don. 3/4-3/5/30.**G.**
Gor. 17/2-22/4/32.**G.**
Gor. 9/8-23/9/32.**L.**
Gor. 4/1-16/2/33.**L.**
Gor. 13/9-27/10/34.**G.**
Don. 19/9-28/11/36.**G.**
Don. 17/6-21/7/38.**G.**
Don. 22/8-20/9/38.**L.**
Don. 18/3-27/4/40.**G.**
Don. 15/4-16/5/43.**G.**
Don. 6/4-25/5/45.**G.**
Don. 18/6-1/8/47.**G.**
Don. 7-11/8/47.**N/C.**
Don. 12-27/2/48.**H.**
Don. 9/9-8/10/48.**H.**
Don. 10/8-21/9/49.**G.**
Don. 1-5/10/49.**N/C.**

BOILERS:
7238.
7513 *(ex3464)* 30/3/26.
7523 *(ex3474)* 3/5/30.
G982 *(ex6287)* 27/10/34.
8461 *(ex2959)* 28/11/36.
4404 *(ex3471)* 25/5/45.
9246 *(ex3480)* 21/9/49.

SHEDS:
New England.
Hornsey 23/6/30.
New England 1/10/30.
Grantham 20/11/42.
New England 12/3/44.
Grantham 30/9/44.
Doncaster 25/6/45.
Frodingham 7/4/46.
Doncaster 18/1/48.
Immingham 30/5/48.
Doncaster 25/6/50.
Retford 18/3/51.

RENUMBERED:
3479 11/9/46.
E3479 27/2/48.
63479 8/10/48.

CONDEMNED:
16/5/51.
Cut up at Doncaster.

3462

N.B.L. 22060.

To traffic 4/1919.

REPAIRS:
Don. 3/5-3/9/21.**G.**
Don. 2/2-21/6/24.**G.** *As 3462.*
Don. 3/5-4/11/26.**G.**
Don. 25/10-22/12/28.**G.**
Don. 15/11/30-25/2/31.**G.**
Gor. 1/4-12/8/33.**G.**
Don. 31/5-13/8/35.**G.**
Don. 8/4-7/7/37.**G.**
Don. 1/8-6/10/39.**G.**
Don. 8/9-23/11/40.**G.** *Air raid damage.*
Don. 4/2-30/3/43.**G.**
Don. 31/1-16/3/45.**G.**
Don. 2/2-8/3/47.**G.**
Don. 26/3-22/4/49.**G.**

BOILERS:
7511.
7717 *(new)* 21/6/24.
7503 *(ex3474)* 12/8/33.
8463 *(ex2961)* 7/7/37.
9246 *(new)* 23/11/40.
9467 *(ex3488)* 22/4/49.

SHEDS:
New England.
Grantham 13/11/42.
Doncaster 25/6/45.

Frodingham 7/4/46.
Doncaster 18/1/48.
Immingham 30/5/48.
Doncaster 25/6/50.
Retford 18/3/51.

RENUMBERED:
3480 27/10/46.
63480 22/4/49.

CONDEMNED:
26/3/51.
Cut up at Doncaster.

3463

N.B.L. 22061.

To traffic 4/1919.

REPAIRS:
Don. 4/5-20/8/21.**G.**
Don. 22/9-15/10/23.**G.** *As 463N.*
Don. 4/1-18/3/26.**G.**
Don. 29/2-23/5/28.**G.**
Don. 23/3-22/5/30.**G.**
Gor. 20/8-3/12/32.**G.**
Gor. 5/3-2/6/34.**G.**

As seen on nos.459 and 474, the original twenty boilers carried Ramsbottom type safety valves and, on the right hand side, had four washout plugs. Replacement boilers began to be fitted from May 1924 and they had 'pop' safety valves, also only three washout plugs.

Don. 13/8-4/10/35.**G.**
Don. 4/11-1/12/37.**G.**
Don. 6/4-13/5/39.**L.**
Don. 6/10-6/12/39.**G.**
Don. 14/12/40-15/1/41.**L.**
Don. 17/12/41-8/2/42.**G.**
Don. 22/4-6/7/43.**G.**
Don. 18/3-5/4/44.**L.**
Don. 21/11-21/12/44.**G.**
Don. 8/2-22/3/47.**G.**
Don. 9/7-9/8/47.**H.**
Don. 6-28/1/49.**G.**

BOILERS:
7512.
7514 *(ex3465)* 18/3/26.
7524 *(ex3475)* 23/5/28.
7525 *(ex3475)* 22/5/30.
7239 *(ex3456)* 3/12/32.
7716 *(ex3467)* 2/6/34.
7505 *(ex3459)* 6/12/39.
7712 *(ex3490)* 8/2/42.
9464 *(new)* 21/12/44.
8458 *(ex3929)* 28/1/49.

SHEDS:
New England.
Grantham 21/11/42.
Doncaster 25/6/45.
Frodingham 7/4/46.
Doncaster 18/1/48.

RENUMBERED:
3481 27/10/46.
63481 28/1/49.

CONDEMNED:
2/4/51.
Cut up at Doncaster.

3464

N.B.L. 22062.

To traffic 5/1919.

REPAIRS:
Don. 6/4-16/7/21.**G.**

Don. 13/6-25/10/24.**G.**
Don. 7/8-2/12/26.**G.**
Don. 5/1-14/3/29.**G.**
Don. 1/1-7/4/31.**G.**
Gor. 2/6-23/9/33.**G.**
Don. 8/5-1/7/35.**G.**
Don. 20/3-27/5/37.*Not repaired.*
Don. 20/9-30/10/37.**G.**
Don. 3/11-15/12/39.**G.**
Don. 26/1-18/4/42.**G.**
Don. 11/5-9/6/44.**G.**
Don. 28/8-29/9/45.**G.**
Don. 4/5-23/7/47.**G.**
Don. 14/5-19/6/50.**G.**

BOILERS:
7513.
7515 *(ex3466)* 25/10/24.
7708 *(ex3494)* 7/4/31.
7504 *(ex3466)* 23/9/33.
7509 *(ex3496)* 15/12/39.
7505 *(ex3463)* 18/4/42.
8184 *(ex3475)* 9/6/44.
9468 *(ex3956)* 19/6/50.

SHEDS:
Colwick.
New England 17/3/25.
Grantham 20/11/42.
Doncaster 25/6/45.
Frodingham 7/4/46.
Doncaster 18/1/48.
Immingham 30/5/48.
Doncaster 25/6/50.
Retford 27/8/50.

(below) **The 1939 war caused this class to be brought within the 13' 0" loading gauge from October 1940 to enable them to be used more widely. The 1' 7^1/$_2$" chimney was replaced by one 3^1/$_2$" shorter, dome cover height was reduced by just over an inch, and the whistle was moved to the front of the cab, instead of on top of it.** *British Railways.*

None of the 20 engines were recorded as being changed from the standard 18" long GNR buffers, but the tender coupled with no.3473 when it suffered this bomb damage in the London Blitz had certainly been changed to Group Standard type by September 1940. Like the people, this tender could "take it" because it served this same engine from August 1934 until December 1950. *L.N.E.R.*

RENUMBERED:
3482 19/5/46.
63482 17/6/50.

CONDEMNED:
21/1/52.
Cut up at Doncaster.

3465

N.B.L. 22063.

To traffic 5/1919.

REPAIRS:
Don. 16/9/21-19/1/22.**G.**
Don. 30/10/24-21/2/25.**G.**

Don. 19/2-2/6/27.**G.**
Don. 9/7-7/9/28.**G.**
Don. 6/12/30-2/3/31.**G.**
Gor. 28/7-11/11/33.**G.**
Don. 15/11-21/12/35.**G.**
Don. 3-17/1/36.**L.**
Don. 28/1-19/3/38.**G.**
Don. 2/3-13/4/40.**G.**
Don. 17/5-27/6/42.**G.**
Don. 21/12/42-10/2/43.**L.** *After collision.*
Don. 2/9-3/10/44.**G.**
Don. 28/12/44-24/1/45.**L.**
Don. 16/5-24/8/46.**G.**
Don. 9/3-15/4/48.**G.**
Don. 13/11-17/12/48.**H.**

BOILERS:
7514.
7511 *(ex3462)* 21/2/25.
7516 *(ex3469)* 2/3/31.
7502 *(ex3475)* 11/11/33.
7690 *(ex3474)* 19/3/38.
8855 *(ex3461)* 13/4/40.
9361 *(new)* 27/6/42.
9162 *(ex3493)* 17/12/48.

SHEDS:
New England.
Doncaster 17/1/36.
Frodingham 7/4/46.
Doncaster 18/1/48.

RENUMBERED:
3483 20/10/46.

63483 15/4/48.

CONDEMNED:
2/4/51.
Cut up at Doncaster.

3466

N.B.L. 22064.

To traffic 5/1919.

REPAIRS:
Don. 7/4-9/7/21.**G.**
Don. 1/1-10/5/24.**G.**
Don. 9/7-24/11/26.**G.**
Don. 8/11/28-11/1/29.**G.**

When no.476 was ex works in November 1922 from its first general repair, it had been fitted with a Worthington feed water heater and pump. From its next general repair, in December 1924, it changed from GNR 476 to LNER 3476, and a larger size of pump had been put on. Another minor change was to the front coupling, the original adjustable screw type having given place to the 3-link loose variety. *L.N.E.R.*

From September 1916, no.459 had carried an additional dome containing collecting trays on to which the cold feed water was pumped when entering the boiler, both domes being enclosed by a single casing. It became 3459 from April 1925, but at its next general repair, when out in June 1927, there had been a change of boiler to one with a normal dome. Note that from its 1925 repair it had lost piston tail rods, although it was into the 1940's before the others lost them. *T.G.Hepburn.*

Don. 19/9-21/11/30.**G.**
Gor. 1/11/32-4/2/33.**G.**
Gor. 20/5-6/10/33.**L.**
Gor. 9/3-31/5/35.**H.**
Don. 9/5-1/7/36.**L.**
Don. 12/2-16/4/37.**G.**
Don. 29/1-25/3/39.**G.**
Don. 24/3-25/4/41.**G.**
Don. 27/3-1/5/43.**G.**
Don. 18/2-3/4/45.**G.**
Don. 29/11/46-4/1/47.**G.**
Don. 6/9-4/10/48.**G.**
Don. 24/10-17/11/50.**G.**
Don. 5/4-1/5/51.**C/L.**

BOILERS:
7515.
7716 *(new)* 10/5/24.
7504 *(ex3480)* 11/1/29.
7525 *(ex3463)* 4/2/33.
8819 *(new)* 31/5/35.
9248 *(new)* 25/4/41.
4402 *(ex3935)* 4/10/48.
21007 *(ex3976)* 17/11/50.

SHEDS:
New England.
Doncaster 14/12/37.
Frodingham 7/4/46.
Doncaster 18/1/48.
Retford 25/2/51.
Doncaster 17/8/52.

RENUMBERED:
3484 20/10/46.
63484 2/10/48.

CONDEMNED:
16/12/52.
Cut up at Doncaster.

3467

N.B.L. 22065.

To traffic 6/1919.

REPAIRS:
Don. 15/10/21-28/1/22.**G.**
Don. 5/4-30/8/24.**G.**
Don. 18/1-28/4/27.**G.**
Don. 9/5-27/6/29.**G.**
Don. 24/2-12/6/31.**G.**
Gor. 28/7-21/10/33.**G.**
Don. 9/7-30/8/35.**G.**
Don. 2/4-15/6/37.**G.**
Don. 26/9-23/11/39.**G.**
Don. 1/12/41-22/1/42.**G.**
Don. 18/3-10/4/42.**L.**
Don. 12/6-29/7/44.**G.**
Don. 1-10/8/44.**N/C.**
Don. 16/6-10/8/46.**G.**
Don. 8/7-19/8/48.**G.**
Don. 14/10-9/11/49.**C/L.**

BOILERS:
7516.
7720 *(new)* 30/8/24.
7716 *(ex3466)* 27/6/29.
7708 *(ex3464)* 21/10/33.
7711 *(ex3488)* 23/11/39.
8857 *(ex3489)* 22/1/42.

8976 *(ex2434)* 29/7/44.
4403 *(ex3470)* 10/8/46.

SHEDS:
New England.
Grantham 20/11/42.
New England 12/3/44.
Grantham 30/9/44.
Doncaster 25/6/45.
Frodingham 7/4/46.
Doncaster 18/1/48.

RENUMBERED:
3485 10/11/46.
63485 19/8/48.

CONDEMNED:
26/9/51.
Cut up at Doncaster.

3468

N.B.L. 22066.

To traffic 6/1919

REPAIRS:
Don. 13/10/21-4/3/22.**G.**
Don. 30/10/24-27/2/25.**G.**
Don. 10/1-7/5/27.**G.**
Don. 26/4-21/6/29.**G.**
Don. 17/12/30-23/2/31.**G.**
Gor. 26/7-8/12/33.**G.**
Don. 15/5-6/7/35.**G.**
Don. 1/4-27/5/37.*Not repaired.*

Don. 19/9-21/10/37.**G.**
Don. 7/3-20/4/40.**G.**
Don. 17/1-20/3/42.**G.**
Don. 2/6-4/7/44.**G.**
Don. 9/7-7/9/46.**G.**
Don. 7/8-18/9/48.**G.**
Don. 1/1/51.*Not repaired.*

BOILERS:
7517.
7512 *(ex3463)* 7/5/27.
7516 *(ex3465)* 8/12/33.
9016 *(new)* 21/10/37.
8461 *(ex3460)* 7/9/46.

SHEDS:
New England.
Colwick 28/11/25.
New England 12/7/29.
Grantham 19/11/42.
Doncaster 25/6/45.
Frodingham 7/4/46.
Doncaster 18/1/48.

RENUMBERED:
3486 17/11/46.
63486 18/9/48.

CONDEMNED:
5/2/51.
Cut up at Doncaster.

Here in the mid-1930's no.3469 still has Ramsbottom safety valves, and also retains the original fittings of piston tail rods, handrails curved round the front of the smokebox, guard irons on both ends of frame and on pony truck, also twin lamp irons at the right hand front corner. The front vacuum standpipe now carries 8 on its load class collar, that having replaced the GN class D1 in the scheme adopted in July 1924 by the LNER for its Southern Area goods engines. *W.H.Whitworth.*

3469

N.B.L. 22067.

To traffic 6/1919.

REPAIRS:
Don. 8/12/21-16/10/22.**G.**
Don. 14/1-25/4/25.**G.**
Don. 17/8-30/11/27.**G.**
Don. 9/4-20/6/30.**G.**
Don. 28/11/31-25/2/32.**G.**
Gor. 29/12/34-2/3/35.**G.**
Don. 11/1-22/3/37.**G.**
Don. 17/4-30/6/39.**G.**
Don. 25/1-22/2/41.**G.**
Don. 7/12/42-3/2/43.**G.**
Don. 7-21/7/44.**H.**
Don. 24/11/46.*Not repaired.*

BOILERS:
7518.
7516 *(ex3467)* 25/4/25.
7234 *(ex3456)* 20/6/30.
7507 *(ex3484)* 2/3/35.
8186 *(ex3487)* 3/2/43.

SHEDS:
Colwick.
New England 13/3/25.
Colwick 27/11/25.
New England 9/8/34.
Colwick 9/10/34.
New England 8/11/34.
Grantham 14/11/42.
Doncaster 25/6/45.

RENUMBERED:
3487 28/9/46.

CONDEMNED:
4/7/47.
Cut up at Doncaster.

3470

N.B.L. 22068.

To traffic 6/1919.

REPAIRS:
Don. 27/3-19/8/22.**G.**
Don. 25/6-18/10/24.**G.**

Don. 15/7-20/11/26.**G.**
Don. 3/3-5/4/27.**L.**
Don. 9/12/28-21/2/29.**G.**
Don. 24/9-25/11/31.**G.**
Gor. 9/11/33-24/2/34.**G.**
Don. 22/11/35-4/1/36.**G.**
Don. 29/12/37-18/1/38.**G.**
Don. 25/3-8/5/40.**G.**
Don. 10-30/7/42.**G.**
Don. 11/1-23/2/45.**G.**
Don. 30/6-21/9/46.**G.**
Don. 17/6-3/8/48.**G.**
Don. 10/6-13/7/50.**G.**
Don. 13/2/52.*For general repair & also conversion to oil burning but partially dismantled prior to temporary use as Stationery Boiler 984 at Hunslet Power House. Returned to Doncaster works 6/53 and cut up.*

BOILERS:
7519.
7719 *(new)* 18/10/24.
7506 *(ex3481)* 25/11/31.
7717 *(ex3462)* 24/2/34.
4403 *(ex2435)* 18/1/38.

9467 *(new)* 23/2/45.
9466 *(ex3954)* 3/8/48.
8184 *(ex3482)* 13/7/50.

SHEDS:
Colwick.
New England 17/3/25.
Grantham 21/11/42.
Doncaster 25/6/45.
Frodingham 7/4/46.
Doncaster 18/1/48.
Retford 3/12/50.

RENUMBERED:
3488 23/9/46.
63488 31/7/48.

CONDEMNED:
22/2/52.
Cut up at Doncaster.

3471

N.B.L. 22069.

To traffic 6/1919.

WORKS CODES:- Cow - Cowlairs. Dar - Darlington. Don - Doncaster. Ghd - Gateshead. Gor - Gorton. Inv - Inverurie. Str - Stratford.

REPAIR CODES:- **C/H** - Casual Heavy. **C/L** - Casual Light. **G** - General. **H** - Heavy. **H/I** - Heavy Intermediate. **L** - Light. **L/I** - Light Intermediate. **N/C** - Non-Classified.

REPAIRS:
Don. 26/7-5/11/21.**G.**
Don. 16/1-28/4/23.**G.**
Don. 15/4-9/8/24.**G.**
Don. 19/10/26-3/2/27.**G.**
Don. 1/12/28-1/2/29.**G.**
Don. 28/7-6/10/30.**G.**
Gor. 28/4-30/9/32.**G.**
Don. 14/8-21/9/34.**G.**
Don. 16/5-15/7/36.**G.**
Don. 19/7-17/8/38.**G.**
Don. 20/5-15/6/40.**G.**
Don. 6/2-16/4/42.**G.**
Don. 24/12/43-29/1/44.**G.**
Don. 12/11-21/12/46.**G.**
Don. 25/6/48.*Not repaired.*

BOILERS:
7520.
7718 *(new)* 9/8/24.
8186 *(new)* 30/9/32.
7714 *(ex3473)* 17/8/38.
4404 *(ex3495)* 15/6/40.
8456 *(ex2435)* 29/1/44.

SHEDS:
Colwick.
New England 16/3/25.
Doncaster 23/11/40.
Grantham 21/11/42.
New England 22/9/44.
Grantham 30/9/44.
Doncaster 25/6/45.
Frodingham 7/4/46.
Doncaster 18/1/48.

RENUMBERED:
3489 10/9/46.

CONDEMNED:
22/7/48.
Cut up at Doncaster.

3472

N.B.L. 22099.

To traffic 10/1919.

REPAIRS:
Don. 20/4-30/9/22.**G.**
Don. 27/10/24-14/2/25.**G.**
Don. 31/10/25-20/2/26.**L.**
Don. 13/5-12/8/27.**G.**
Don. 10/11/29-15/1/30.**G.**
Gor. 4/10/32-21/1/33.**G.**
Gor. 12/10-24/11/34.**G.**
Don. 14/9-16/10/36.**G.**
Don. 26/8-29/9/38.**G.**
Don. 26/7-4/9/40.**G.**
Don. 12/4-6/6/41.**L.**
Don. 11/4-16/5/43.**G.**
Don. 13/6-1/8/45.**G.**
Don. 21/5-17/7/46.**G.**
Don. 25/5/47.*Not repaired.*

BOILERS:
7521.
7517 *(ex3468)* 12/8/27.
7523 *(ex3460)* 24/11/34.
8182 *(ex3490)* 29/9/38.
8185 *(ex3475)* 4/9/40.
8458 *(ex2958)* 16/5/43.

SHEDS:
New England.
Grantham 21/11/42.
Doncaster 1/8/45.
Frodingham 7/4/46.

RENUMBERED:
3490 17/11/46.

CONDEMNED:
19/6/47.*Cut up at Doncaster.*

3473

N.B.L. 22100.

To traffic 10/1919.

REPAIRS:
Don. 21/3-25/8/22.**G.**
Don. 26/7-22/11/24.**G.**
Don. 23/1-14/2/25.**L.**
Don. 1/4-20/7/27.**G.**
Don. 17/8-25/10/29.**G.**
Gor. 19/1-30/4/32.**G.**
Gor. 19/6-25/8/34.**G.**
Don. 29/3-9/5/36.**G.**
Don. 10/8-25/9/37.**L.**
Don. 3/7-3/8/38.**G.**
Don. 3/7-14/8/40.**G.**
Don. 9/9-20/12/40.**H.***Air raid damage.*
Don. 25/1-3/3/43.**G.**
Don. 25/8-23/9/44.**G.**
Don. 28/10-7/12/46.**G.**
Don. 20/10-6/12/48.**G.**
Don. 11/1-14/2/49.**C/L.**
Don. 24/11/50.*Not repaired.*

BOILERS:
7522.
7235 *(ex3457)* 20/7/27.
7714 *(ex3500)* 25/8/34.
7707 *(ex3477)* 3/8/38.
8460 *(ex2432)* 14/8/40.
8822 *(ex3482)* 7/12/46.

SHEDS:
New England.
Grantham 21/11/42.
Doncaster 25/6/45.
Frodingham 7/4/46.
Doncaster 18/1/48.

RENUMBERED:
3491 17/11/46.
63491 4/12/48.

CONDEMNED:
18/12/50.
Cut up at Doncaster.

3474

N.B.L. 22101.

To traffic 10/1919.

REPAIRS:
Don. 18/1-13/5/22.**G.**
Don. 12/8-29/11/24.**G.**
Don. 20/4-30/5/25.**L.**
Don. 9/7-9/11/26.**G.**
Don. 23/9-1/12/28.**G.**
Don. 13/11/30-22/1/31.**G.**
Gor. 19/12/32-31/3/33.**G.**
Gor. 15/5-7/7/33.**L.**
Gor. 3/1-23/2/35.**G.**
Don. 27/11/35-15/1/36.**G.**
Don. 20/12/37-15/1/38.**G.**
Don. 11/12/39-5/2/40.**G.**
Don. 20/12/41-12/2/42.**G.**
Don. 10/11-23/12/42.**L.***After collision.*
Don. 7/4-6/5/44.**G.**
Don. 23/9-26/10/45.**G.**
Don. 22/3/47.*Not repaired.*

BOILERS:
7523.
7505 *(ex3481)* 1/12/28.
7503 *(ex3479)* 22/1/31.
7521 *(ex3458)* 31/3/33.
7690 *(ex3456)* 23/2/35.
4402 *(ex2436)* 15/1/38.

3468 seen ex works in September 1946 has lost load class collar, but had L8 painted on the buffer beam; it had also regained LNER on its tender from the wartime contraction to just NE. Note piston rods have been removed, and the boiler handrails are now cut back from front to side of the smokebox. *L.N.E.R.*

3474 continued
9013 *(ex2959)* 6/5/44.

SHEDS:
New England.
Doncaster 22/1/38.
Grantham 6/5/45.
Doncaster 25/6/45.
Frodingham 7/4/46.

RENUMBERED:
3492 17/11/46.

CONDEMNED:
10/5/47.
Cut up at Doncaster.

3475

N.B.L. 22102.

To traffic 10/1919.

REPAIRS:
Don. 16/2-19/6/22.**G.**
Don. 28/11/24-11/4/25.**G.**
Don. 9/7-1/12/27.**G.**
Don. 12/3-10/5/30.**G.**
Gor. 11/11/32-18/2/33.**G.**

Don. 15/11-23/12/35.**G.**
Don. 11/12/37-7/1/38.**G.**
Don. 29/6-26/7/40.**G.**
Don. 3/7-14/8/42.**G.**
Don. 28/5-21/6/43.**G.**
Don. 3/10-3/11/44.**H.**
Don. 11/12/44-4/1/45.**H.**
Don. 16/7-26/9/46.**G.**
Don. 22/1-24/3/47.**L.**
Don. 12/6-22/7/48.**G.**
Don. 5/11-13/12/49.**C/L.**

BOILERS:
7524.
7525 *(ex3476)* 1/12/27.
7502 *(ex3478)* 10/5/30.
7718 *(ex3471)* 18/2/33.
8185 *(ex3498)* 7/1/38.
8184 *(ex3499)* 26/7/40.
8856 *(ex3486)* 21/6/43.
9162 *(ex3495)* 4/1/45.
8182 *(ex3491)* 22/7/48.

SHEDS:
New England.
Colwick 27/11/25.
New England 9/8/34.
Colwick 8/10/34.
New England 8/11/34.
Doncaster 23/11/40.

Frodingham 7/4/46.
Doncaster 18/1/48.

RENUMBERED:
3493 15/12/46.
63493 22/7/48.

CONDEMNED:
19/2/51.
Cut up at Doncaster.

3476

N.B.L. 22103.

To traffic 10/1919.

REPAIRS:
Don. 18/4-18/11/22.**G.**
Worthington pump on.
Don. 27/6-5/12/24.**G.**
Don. 23/5-23/6/26.**G.**
Don. 18/1-12/5/27.**G.**
Worthington pump off.
Don. 9/8-26/9/29.**G.** *Silvertow*
mech.lub.
Gor. 22/3-25/6/32.**G.**
Gor. 9/5-7/7/34.**G.**
Don. 8/5-2/7/36.**G.**

Don. 23/5-8/7/38.**G.**
Don. 31/1-2/3/40.**L.**
Don. 21/7-28/8/40.**G.**
Don. 29/9-5/11/42.**G.**
Don. 27/10-27/11/44.**G.**
Don. 18/2-30/3/46.**L.**
Don. 30/8-19/10/46.**G.**
Don. 17/2/48.*Not repaired.*

BOILERS:
7525.
7520 *(ex3471)* 12/5/27.
7720 *(ex3467)* 26/9/29.
7510 *(ex3486)* 25/6/32.
G982 *(ex3495)* 8/7/38.
9462 *(new)* 27/11/44.

SHEDS:
New England.
Doncaster 12/7/39.
Frodingham 7/4/46.
Doncaster 18/1/48.

RENUMBERED:
3494 27/10/46.

CONDEMNED:
5/3/48.
Cut up at Doncaster.

Interchanging of boilers with O2 class led to O1 class being seen with 4 washout plugs, and 'pop' safety valves, no.3475 here carrying 478's original boiler, from May 1930 to November 1932. The tender then coupled was of the early class B type which had equally spaced axles, and a hand grip at the front end. This one was tender no.988, which had been built in June 1900. *W.L.Good.*

In 1924/25, when LNER painting and numbering was being applied, all twenty were then coupled with the earlier type class B tender on which the coal capacity was 5¹/2 tons. As shown here by 3465 they were required to do the same work as the later O2 class engines, although the latter had the benefit of tenders carrying 6¹/2 tons of coal. In 1923 some of those earlier tenders had an extra coal rail added, one of them running with 3460 from March to May 1936, but 3457 had the benefit of one of them from July 1933 until April 1946.

During the later 1920's, when bad weather affected them, it was found that O1 class with the 5¹/2 tons coal capacity tender were having to call at Hitchin to take on more coal. On 31st January 1929 an instruction was issued that these 5¹/2 tons tenders were to be replaced on O1 class by the later 6¹/2 ton type, and here ex works on 14th March 1929, No.3464 has been so changed. Note that it still has tail rods, but the long-redundant extra lamp iron has been removed, and that it has also lost the load class collar from its vacuum standpipe.

462 to 471 were built by the Hyde Park works of N.B.Loco.Co who painted them grey with white lining. Concerned with building only the engine, they centred the running number on the full height of the cab, which did not match the level of the GNR on the tender with which it was coupled on completion. Nor did the painting match, because the tender Doncaster supplied was unlined. *W.H.Whitworth.*

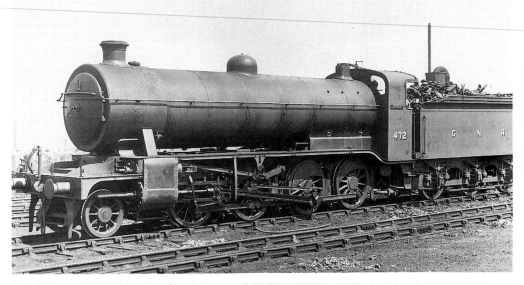

The other five were built by N.B.Loco.Co at their Atlas works and the discrepancy in levels had been noticed in time for them not to be led astray. During 1920/21, the higher number position on the first ten was duly corrected.

After the Grouping, standard painting became black with single red lining, no.471 being the first to get it, and also the only one to have L&NER on tender. 457, 460, and 463 did not have the ampersand, but were the only three to have the suffix N applied, before the change to adding 3000 to the number began on 3458 ex works 11th February 1924, completion being made by 3469 on 25th April 1925. The June 1928 economies in painting caused the loss of the red lining, and from early 1929 the running number reverted from tender to cab side.

The same German bomb which damaged the tender 3473 had a rather more drastic effect on 3462 which was standing behind that tender at Hornsey in September 1940. Both were restored and back in traffic well before the end of the year. A side effect of the damage gives us a clear view of the piston tail rod. *L.N.E.R.*

During 1946 the whole class was renumbered to 3475-94 in order of building date, and from January it had been possible to use LNER again, applied by shaded transfers until September when 3468 was the last O1 so adorned. Their cost was considered prohibitive, so a change was made to yellow painted, and unlined, Gill Sans. This picture shows 3482 (formerly 3464) at Sheffield Darnall shed on 4th September 1949, and is typical of the neglected appearance to which the class had been allowed to drift. Identification is just possible on front buffer beam.

Doncaster built no.460 worked its first 28 years shuttling between Peterborough and London on trains of which this was typical. In addition to the long string of empty coal wagons, four cattle wagons - also empty - have been tucked in. *Lens of Sutton.*

No.472, one of the Scottish built engines, is also returning coal wagons to be loaded again, and like the engine, to do the same job all over again. *Lens of Sutton.*

Numbered 3457 from April 1926, and here approaching Potters Bar, another typical O1 hauled load is on its way to London. Note the varying heights of the leading 13 coal wagons, some of the coal no doubt destined for passenger engines at King's Cross shed, the following portion of the train being very mixed general goods.

A mineral engine fitted with indicator shelter was a rare sight indeed. 3466 here in February 1925 is leaving Wood Green tunnel on the 10.15 a.m. Clarence Yard to Peterborough whilst in course of trials for comparison with O2 class no.3479.

Not until during the 1939-45 war were O1 activities more widely spread, and here on 15th September 1945, no.3473 by then shedded at Doncaster, is at Guide Bridge with a load of coal for Lancashire power stations from collieries in South Yorkshire, work with which it was only too familiar. *H.C.Casserley.*

It is not easy now to recall that the London demand for coal was not all for industrial use, but that enormous amounts were consumed in household grates. Here in early 1928 no.3475 has a full load of coal in private owners' wagons many of them stridently proclaiming to whom they belong, names such as JUDBUD conjuring up many familiar memories of GN main line sightings. *W.L.Good.*

Before the class disappeared, some of them did get rather improved treatment, 63482 in June 1950 being one of the seven to acquire the small size B.R. emblem on their tender. Applied from September 1949 to November 1950, those to be so treated were nos 63475, 63476, 63478, 63479, 63482, 63484 and 63488.

63476 was withdrawn on 17th March 1952, and on a Sunday three weeks later is here in the scrap yard at Doncaster works. It was not all gloom however, because the boiler was recovered, and subsequently served on no less than three engines of O2 class, surviving until condemned in July 1961. *A.B.Crompton.*

Prior to losing their identity at Grouping, the GNR added ten more numbered 477 to 486, on which the outside cylinders were in the more orthodox horizontal position and the valve gear for the middle cylinder took up the forward location for it. In due course, the LNER allocated Part 1 to those ten, with 461 simply as O2. Another change was the adoption of 'pop' safety valves as standard instead of the Ramsbottom type, but they were still to the generous 13' 4" maximum height from rail.

A further fifteen engines were soon added, and to give them wider capability of use their dimensions were brought within the Composite Load Gauge which had been promulgated, the shorter chimney, and moving the whistle from top to front of cab being clearly apparent. That put them into Part 2 of the class, and their dates into traffic spanned the period when the LNER were still uncertain how to number. 487 to 501 had been allocated to them, but they began as 487N to 495N and 3496 to 3501. *L.N.E.R.*

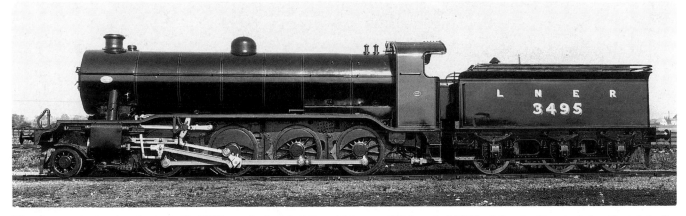

The first twenty engines began with GNR numbering, but from February 1924 needed 3000 adding to them to bring them into the system the LNER had adopted. From April 1924 on 3479, it took until October 1926 when 3495 completed that change. The standard painting was black, with single red lining, well shown in this picture. *British Railways.*

CLASS 02

3461

Doncaster 1481.

To traffic 5/1918.

REPAIRS:
Don. 30/4-3/7/20.**G.**
Don. 9/5-10/10/23.**G.** *As 461N.*
To 3461 on 9/3/25.
Don. 7/6-16/10/26.**G.**
Don. 28/11/28-2/2/29.**G.**
Double dome boiler.
Don. 31/12/29-15/2/30.**L.**
Don. 6/2-12/3/32.**G.**
Don. 14/10-18/11/33.**G.**
F.W.H.in double dome.
Don. 5/10-2/11/35.**G.** *Double
dome removed.*
Don. 3/7-9/10/37.**G.**
Don. 10/2-30/3/40.**G.** *S.W.cab
fitted.*
Don. 31/1-7/3/42.**G.**
Don. 22/4-20/5/44.**G.**
Don. 13/1-3/2/45.**L.**
Don. 20/10-10/11/45.**G.**

BOILERS:
7239.
7518 *(ex3469)* 16/10/26.
7237 *(ex3459)* 2/2/29.
8855 *(new)* 2/11/35.
9164 *(new)* 30/3/40.
8821 *(ex3485)* 10/11/45.

SHEDS:
New England.
Doncaster 11/5/43.
Colwick 23/1/44.
New England 24/12/44.
Colwick 25/6/45.
Doncaster 2/12/45.
Langwith 27/10/46.

RENUMBERED:
3921 27/7/46.

CONDEMNED:
21/5/48.
Cut up at Doncaster.

3477

N.B.L. 22691.

To traffic 4/1921.

REPAIRS:
Don. 20/3-16/7/23.**G.**
Don. 27/9-6/10/23.**L.**
Don. 27/3-4/7/25.**G.**
Don. 27/5-26/8/27.**G.**
Don. 27/8-21/12/27.**L.**
Don. 9/11-21/12/29.**G.**
Don. 7/11-19/12/31.**G.**
Don. 3-31/3/34.**G.**
Don. 25/1-15/2/36.**G.**
Don. 6/6-4/7/36.**H.**
Don. 25/6-16/7/38.**G.**
Don. 18/5-15/6/40.**G.** *S.W.cab
fitted.*
Don. 16/5-20/6/42.**G.**
Don. 22/4-10/5/44.**G.**
Don. 23/3/46-10/7/47.**G.**
Don. 9/11-2/12/49.**G.**
Don. 5/7-3/8/51.**G.**
Don. 28/3-26/4/54.**G.**
Don. 13/6-26/7/56.**G.**
Don. 22/10-29/11/58.**G.**
Don. 12-21/8/59.**N/C.**
Don. 8/8-19/9/61.**G.**
Don. 2/11/62.*Not repaired.*

BOILERS:
7501.
7520 *(ex3476)* 21/12/39.
7707 *(ex3493)* 31/3/34.
7713 *(ex3456)* 16/7/38.
8819 *(ex3466)* 20/6/42.
9366 *(ex3952)* 2/12/49.
21031 *(ex3479)* 3/8/51.
21042 *(ex3980)* 26/4/54.
21024 *(ex3983)* 26/7/56.
21023 *(ex3926)* 29/11/58.

SHEDS:
New England.
Doncaster 14/5/43.
Colwick 23/1/44.
New England 24/12/44.
Colwick 25/6/45.
Doncaster 9/12/45.
Frodingham 20/10/47.
Doncaster 13/6/54.
Grantham 29/7/62.

RENUMBERED:
3922 28/9/46.
63922 2/12/49.

CONDEMNED:
5/11/62.
Cut up at Doncaster.

3478

N.B.L. 22692.

To traffic 4/1921.

REPAIRS:
Don. 21/3-9/7/23.**G.** *LNER.*
Don. 2/9-21/11/25.**G.**
Don. 3/12/27-3/3/28.**G.**
Don. 14/12/29-18/1/30.**G.**
Don. 20/2-26/3/32.**G.**
Don. 7/4-5/5/34.**G.**
Don. 4/4-2/5/36.**G.**
Don. 23-30/5/36.**L.**
Don. 9/7-13/8/38.**G.**
Don. 22/6-13/7/40.**G.** *S.W.cab
fitted.*
Don. 5/9-3/10/42.**G.**
Don. 6-20/11/43.**L.**
Don. 27/5-17/6/44.**G.**
Don. 5-26/1/46.**L.**
Don. 3-24/8/46.**G.**
Don. 1/8-1/9/48.**G.**
Don. 22/10-17/11/50.**G.**
Don. 10/3-8/4/53.**G.**
Don. 19/1-17/2/55.**G.**
Don. 27/11-21/12/57.**G.**
Don. 13/7-12/8/60.**G.**

BOILERS:
7502.
7518 *(ex3461)* 18/1/30.
7712 *(ex3498)* 5/5/34.
8975 *(ex2959)* 13/8/38.
8859 *(ex3498)* 24/8/46.
9239 *(ex3940)* 1/9/48.
21006 *(ex3957)* 17/11/50.
21065 *(ex3957)* 8/4/53.
21054 *(ex3937)* 17/2/55.
21011 *(ex3971)* 21/12/57.
21030 *(ex3930)* 12/8/60.

SHEDS:
New England.
Doncaster 12/5/43.
Colwick 23/1/44.
New England 24/12/44.
Colwick 25/6/45.
Doncaster 9/12/45.

Langwith 27/10/46.
Grantham 18/6/50.
New England 20/8/50.
Grantham 11/3/51.

RENUMBERED:
3923 24/8/46.
63923 1/9/48.

29/12/62.
*Sold for scrap to Central Wagon
Co. Ince.*

3479

N.B.L. 22693.

To traffic 6/1921.

REPAIRS:
Don. 14/11/23-5/4/24.**G.**
Don. 10/1-9/2/25.**L.**
Don. 12/7-18/11/26.**G.**
Don. 3/8-5/10/28.**G.**
Don. 7/6-19/7/30.**G.**
Don. 21/1-18/2/33.**G.**
Don. 30/9-14/10/33.**L.**
Don. 16/3-6/4/35.**G.**
Don. 27/3-17/4/37.**G.**
Don. 1/7-5/8/39.**G.** *S.W.cab
fitted.*
Don. 3/5-14/6/41.**G.**
Don. 17/7-2/10/43.**G.**
Don. 21-28/4/45.**L.**
Don. 31/8-5/10/46.**G.**
Don. 8/10-5/11/48.**G.**
Don. 3-31/7/51.**G.**
Don. 25/3-23/4/54.**G.**
Don. 28/6-4/8/56.**G.**
Don. 25/4-27/5/59.**G.**
Don. 15-24/10/59.**N/C.**
Don. 29/12/61-31/1/62.**G.**

BOILERS:
7503.
7524 *(ex3463)* 19/7/30.
8820 *(new)* 6/4/35.
9435 *(new)* 2/10/43.
28156 *(ex3950)* 31/7/51.
28111 *(ex61379)* 23/4/54.
28436 *(ex1070)* 27/5/59.

SHEDS:
New England.

WORKS CODES:- Cow - Cowlairs. Dar - Darlington. Don - Doncaster. Ghd - Gateshead. Gor - Gorton. Inv - Inverurie. Str - Stratford.

REPAIR CODES:- **C/H** - Casual Heavy. **C/L** - Casual Light. **G** - General. **H** - Heavy. **H/I** - Heavy Intermediate. **L** - Light. **L/I** - Light Intermediate. **N/C** - Non-Classified.

29

In the early 1930's the London coal traffic warranted the building of further class O2, especially for use on the former Great Eastern main line. Sixteen to take numbers 2954 to 2961 and 2430 to 2437 duly appeared from Doncaster, and were given Part 3, because they differed by being provided with more commodious and side-window cab. For the first twelve, 4200 gallon Group Standard tender was taken from J38 class in Scottish Area which, when built in 1926, were to the design with stepped-out top. *A.G.Ellis.*

Doncaster 13/5/43.
Colwick 23/1/44.
New England 21/9/44.
Colwick 25/6/45.
Doncaster 9/12/45.
Langwith 27/10/46.
Mexborough 18/6/50.
Retford 14/9/52.

RENUMBERED:
3924 16/6/46.
63924 5/11/48.

CONDEMNED:
3/11/63.
Cut up at Doncaster.

3480

N.B.L. 22694.

To traffic 6/1921.

REPAIRS:
Don. 18/4-1/9/23.**G.** *As 480N.*
Don. 27/2-3/7/26.**G.**
Don. 3/10-12/12/28.**G.**
Don. 18/10-29/11/30.**G.**
Don. 15/4-20/5/33.**G.**
Don. 23/3-13/4/35.**G.**
Don. 20/2-20/3/37.**G.**
Don. 25/2-8/4/39.**G.**
Don. 21/9-26/10/40.**G.**
S.W.cab fitted.

Don. 6/3-3/4/43.**G.**
Don. 21/4-26/5/45.**G.**
Don. 18/5-23/6/47.**G.**
Don. 6/4-4/5/49.**G.**
Don. 18/7-5/8/49.**C/L.**
Don. 5/6-5/7/51.**G.**
Don. 5-31/7/53.**G.**
Don. 9/11-10/12/55.**G.**
Don. 29/5-15/7/58.**G.**
Don. 16/11-20/12/60.**G.**
Don. 2-18/10/61.**C/L.**

BOILERS:
7504.
7509 *(ex3485)* 12/12/28.
7706 *(ex3492)* 20/5/33.
7709 *(ex3492)* 26/10/40.
9465 *(new)* 26/5/45.
9464 *(ex3481)* 4/5/49.
21027 *(ex3981)* 5/7/51.
21019 *(ex3926)* 31/7/53.
21033 *(ex3927)* 10/12/55.
28354 *(ex1659)* 15/7/58.
28577 *(ex61360)* 20/12/60.

SHEDS:
New England.
Doncaster 15/5/43.
Colwick 23/1/44.
New England 21/12/44.
Colwick 25/6/45.
Doncaster 5/12/45.
Langwith 27/10/46.
Doncaster 25/6/50.
Retford 3/2/52.

RENUMBERED:
3925 20/10/46.
63925 4/5/49.

CONDEMNED:
8/9/63.
Sold for scrap to Bulwell Forest Wagon Works.

3481

N.B.L. 22695.

To traffic 6/1921.

REPAIRS:
Don. 31/5-29/10/23.**G.** *As 481N.*
To 3481 on 9/3/25.
Don. 10/12/25-26/2/26.**G.**
Don. 17/4-10/8/28.**G.**
Don. 30/8-4/10/30.**G.**
Don. 26/11-24/12/32.**G.**
Don. 22/12/34-19/1/35.**G.**
Don. 3-24/10/36.**G.**
Don. 5-26/11/38.**G.**
Don. 7/9-12/10/40.**G.** *S.W.cab fitted.*
Don. 1/5-5/6/43.**G.**
Don. 5-19/2/44.**L.**
Don. 7/7-18/8/45.**G.**
Don. 22/12/46-1/2/47.**G.**
Don. 15/9-28/10/48.**G.**
Don. 25/9-11/10/49.**C/H.**
Don. 11/3-12/4/51.**G.**

Don. 2/6-8/7/53.**G.**
Don. 10/7-11/8/55.**G.**
Don. 19/11-22/12/56.**C/L.**
Don. 27/5-11/7/58.**G.**
Don. 1/2-9/3/61.**G.**
Don. 30/1-23/2/62.**C/L.**
Don. 9-20/7/62.**C/L.**

BOILERS:
7505.
7506 *(ex3482)* 10/8/28.
7513 *(ex3460)* 4/10/30.
7720 *(ex3476)* 24/12/32.
9243 *(new)* 12/10/40.
8858 *(ex spare and 2961)* 28/10/48.
8975 *(ex3973)* 11/10/49.
21019 *(ex3468)* 12/4/51.
21023 *(ex3971)* 8/7/53.
21002 *(ex3958)* 11/7/58.
28564 *(ex1181)* 9/3/61.

SHEDS:
New England.
Doncaster 13/6/43.
Colwick 19/2/44.
New England 17/1/45.
Colwick 25/6/45.
Doncaster 5/12/45.
Langwith 27/10/46.
Doncaster 25/6/50.
Retford 3/2/52.

RENUMBERED:
3926 19/10/46.

63926 28/10/48.

CONDEMNED:
22/9/63.
Sold for scrap to Bulwell Forest Wagon Works.

3482

N.B.L 22696..

To traffic 6/1921.

REPAIRS:
Don. 14/6-27/10/23.**G.**
Don. 2/9-12/12/25.**G.**
Don. 16/2-3/5/28.**G.**
Don. 12/7-9/8/30.**G.**
Don. 11/3-8/4/33.**G.** *Diamond soot blower on.*
Don. 4/5-1/6/35.**G.**
Don. 19/6-21/8/37.**G.**
Don. 16/9-4/11/39.**G.** *S.W.cab fitted.*
Don. 8/11-13/12/41.**G.**
Don. 28/11-12/12/42.**L.**
Don. 22/1-19/2/44.**G.**
Don. 3/11-1/12/45.**G.**
Don. 11/5-8/6/47.**G.**
Don. 10/6-15/7/49.**G.**
Don. 7-30/5/50.**C/L.**
Don. 26/6-27/7/51.**G.**
Don. 26/8-2/10/53.**G.**
Don. 1/11-1/12/55.**G.**
Don. 14-25/5/57.**C/L.**
Don. 9/10-13/11/58.**G.**
Don. 20/7-1/8/59.**N/C.**
Don. 3/10-24/11/61.**G.**
Don. 7/1-8/2/63.**C/L.**

BOILERS:
7506.
7522 *(ex3473)* 3/5/28.
8822 *(new)* 1/6/35.
9015 *(ex3488)* 1/12/45.
8459 *(ex3946)* 15/7/49.
21030 *(ex3925)* 27/7/51.
21033 *(ex3978)* 2/10/53.
21063 *(ex3957)* 1/12/55.
21031 *(ex3985)* 13/11/58.
21027 *(ex3973)* 24/11/61.

SHEDS:
New England.
Doncaster 13/6/43.
Colwick 19/2/44.
New England 17/1/45.
Colwick 25/6/45.
Doncaster 5/12/45.
Langwith 27/10/46.
Mexborough 2/7/50.
Doncaster 25/2/51.

Retford 17/2/52.

RENUMBERED:
3927 13/5/46.
63927 15/7/49.

CONDEMNED:
22/9/63.
Sold for scrap to Bulwell Forest Wagon Works.

3483

N.B.L. 22697.

To traffic 7/1921.

REPAIRS:
Don. 14/6-7/11/23.**G.** *As 483N. To 3483 5/25.*
Don. 18/12/25-26/3/26.**G.**
Don. 29/2-18/5/28.**G.**
Don. 11/1-8/2/30.**G.**
Don. 26/3-23/4/32.**G.**
Don. 16/6-14/7/34.**G.**
Don. 11/7-8/8/36.**G.**
Don. 6-20/8/38.**G.**
Don. 27/4-25/5/40.**G.** *S.W.cab fitted.*
Don. 15/8-12/9/42.**G.**
Don. 7/10-11/11/44.**G.**
Don. 12-26/10/46.**G.**
Don. 11/7-23/8/48.**G.**
Don. 26/2-7/3/50.**C/L.**
Don. 9/1-1/2/51.**G.**
Don. 10/2-3/5/52.**C/L.**
Don. 21/5-30/6/53.**G.**
Don. 18/5-28/6/55.**G.**
Don. 29/11/57-4/1/58.**G.**
Don. 10-24/9/59.**N/C.**
Don. 2/6-15/7/61.**G.**

BOILERS:
7505.
7236 *(ex3458)* 8/2/30.
8973 *(new)* 8/8/36.
8185 *(ex3472)* 11/11/44.
21013 *(ex3942)* 1/2/51.
21014 *(ex3933)* 30/6/53.
21003 *(ex3931)* 28/6/55.
28595 *(ex61314)* 15/7/61.

SHEDS:
New England.
Doncaster 6/9/43.
Colwick 23/1/44.
New England 17/1/45.
Colwick 25/6/45.
Doncaster 9/12/45.
Langwith 24/11/46.
Doncaster 25/6/50.
Grantham 26/11/61.

RENUMBERED:
3928 1/8/46.
63928 21/8/48.

CONDEMNED:
8/9/63.
Sold for scrap to Bulwell Forest Wagon Works.

3484

N.B.L. 22698.

To traffic 7/1921.

REPAIRS:
Don. 12-16/7/21.**L.**
Don. 29/1/23.**N/C.** *Specimen L&NER painting.*
Don. 29/8-27/11/23.**G.** *As 484N.*
Don. 10/2-19/5/26.**G.**
Don. 28/5-17/8/28.**G.**
Don. 6/9-18/10/30.**G.**
Don. 20/2-26/3/32.**G.**
Don. 7/4-5/5/34.**G.**
Don. 18/4-16/5/36.**G.**
Don. 21/5-13/8/38.**G.**
Don. 13/7-10/8/40.**G.** *SW.cab fitted.*
Don. 27/6-25/7/42.**G.**
Don. 12/8-9/9/44.**G.**
Don. 10-31/8/46.**G.**
Don. 11/11-3/12/47.**H.**
Don. 15/10-15/11/48.**G.**
Don. 8/4-8/5/51.**G.**
Don. 19/5-15/6/54.**G.**
Don. 19/6-28/7/56.**G.**
Don. 3/6-10/7/59.**G.**
Don. 19/8-1/9/60.**N/C.**

BOILERS:
7508.
7507 *(ex3483)* 18/10/30.
7710 *(ex3496)* 5/5/34.
9241 *(new)* 10/8/40.
8458 *(ex3490)* 3/12/47.
9389 *(ex3977)* 15/11/48.
21022 *(ex3949)* 8/5/51.
21047 *(ex3985)* 15/6/54.
28957 *(new)* 10/7/59.

SHEDS:
New England.
Doncaster 6/9/43.
Colwick 23/1/44.
New England 17/1/45.
Grantham 25/6/45.

RENUMBERED:
3929 31/8/46.
63929 13/11/48.

CONDEMNED:
9/7/62.
Cut up at Doncaster.

3485

N.B.L. 22699.

To traffic 7/1921.

REPAIRS:
Don. 15/8-10/11/23.**G.** *As 485N.*
Don. 13/11/25-28/1/26.**G.**
Don. 18/5-16/8/28.**G.**
Don. 20/9-1/11/30.**G.**
Don. 18/3-29/4/33.**G.** *Diamond soot blower on.*
Don. 6/4-4/5/35.**G.**
Don. 3/4-1/5/37.**G.**
Don. 29/4-10/6/39.**G.** *S.W.cab fitted.*
Don. 12/4-10/5/41.**G.**
Don. 15/5-13/6/43.**G.**
Don. 18/11-16/12/44.**G.**
Don. 7/11-21/12/46.**G.**
Don. 16/3-29/4/48.**G.**
Don. 24-26/1/49.**N/C.**
Don. 2/10-8/11/50.**G.**
Don. 5/9-2/10/53.**G.**
Don. 19/4-25/5/56.**G.**
Don. 23/7-19/8/59.**G.**

BOILERS:
7509.
7514 *(ex3463)* 16/8/28.
7513 *(ex3481)* 29/4/33.
8821 *(new)* 4/5/35.
9463 *(new)* 16/12/44.
8186 *(ex3469)* 29/4/48.
21005 *(ex3955)* 8/11/50.
21030 *(ex3974)* 25/5/56.
28961 *(new)* 19/8/59.

SHEDS:
New England.
Doncaster 5/9/43.
Colwick 23/1/44.
New England 17/1/45.
Grantham 25/6/45.

RENUMBERED:
3930 1/9/46.
63930 29/4/48.

CONDEMNED:
29/12/62. Sold for scrap to Central Wagon Co.Ince.

3486	3487	3488	3489
N.B.L. 22700.	Doncaster 1574.	Doncaster 1575.	Doncaster 1576.
To traffic 7/1921.	To traffic 1/11/23 as 487N.	To traffic 3/11/23.	To traffic 14/11/23.

3486

N.B.L. 22700.

To traffic 7/1921.

REPAIRS:
Don. 5/9-15/12/23.**G.** *As 486N.*
Don. 1/12/25-13/2/26.**G.**
Don. 19/1-14/4/28.**G.**
Don. 23/9-30/11/28.**G.**
Don. 27/4-8/6/29.**G.**
Don. 3-31/10/31.**G.**
Don. 10/2-17/3/34.**G.**
Don. 8/2-7/3/36.**G.**
Don. 26/2-26/3/38.**G.**
Don. 13/4-18/5/40.**G.** S.W.cab
fitted.
Don. 23/1-20/3/43.**G.**
Don. 27/1-10/3/45.**G.**
Don. 11/4-24/5/47.**G.**
Don. 22/10-24/11/49.**G.**
Don. 24/7-31/8/52.**G.**
Don. 9/5-1/6/53.**C/L.**
Don. 5/5-3/6/55.**G.**
Don. 7/1-1/2/58.**G.**
Don. 20/11/61-6/1/62.**G.**

BOILERS:
7510.
7508 *(ex3484)* 31/10/31.
8856 *(new)* 7/3/36.
9365 *(new)* 20/3/43.
9385 *(ex3973)* 24/5/47.
9463 *(ex3940)* 24/11/49.
21003 *(ex3946)* 31/8/52.
21008 *(ex3971)* 3/6/55.
21032 *(ex3966)* 1/2/58.
28531 *(ex1107)* 6/1/62.

SHEDS:
New England.
Doncaster 5/9/43.
Colwick 23/1/44.
New England 29/3/44.
Grantham 25/6/45.
Doncaster 8/9/63.

RENUMBERED:
3931 1/9/46.
63931 24/11/49.

CONDEMNED:
22/9/63.
Cut up at Doncaster.

3487

Doncaster 1574.

To traffic 1/11/23 as 487N.

REPAIRS:
Don. 14/1-3/3/25.**L.** *to 3487.*
Don. 24/1-16/4/27.**G.**
Don. 23/3-11/5/29.**G.**
Don. 4/4-9/5/31.**G.**
Don. 22/10-3/12/32.**G.**
Don. 21/1-4/2/33.**L.**
Don. 1-29/9/34.**G.**
Don. 22/8-26/9/36.**G.**
Don. 13/8-3/9/38.**G.**
Don. 7/9-12/10/40.**G.**
Don. 15/8-12/9/42.**G.**
Don. 30/9-28/10/44.**G.**
Don. 4/11-21/12/46.**G.**
Don. 10/5-7/6/49.**G.**
Don. 24/11-19/12/51.**G.**
Don. 25/1-24/2/55.**G.**
Don. 25/3-2/5/58.**G.**
Don. 15-30/9/60.**N/C.**
Don. 16/2-23/3/62.**G.**

BOILERS:
7688.
7511 *(ex3465)* 9/5/31.
7692 *(ex3491)* 29/9/34.
8186 *(ex3488)* 12/10/40.
4405 *(ex2432)* 12/9/42.
9444 *(new)* 28/10/44.
9397 *(ex3985)* 7/6/49.
21044 *(ex3977)* 19/12/51.
21065 *(ex3923)* 24/2/55.
28171 *(ex1666)* 2/5/58.
28404 *(ex1281)* 23/3/62.

SHEDS:
New England.
Doncaster 9/9/43.
Colwick 23/1/44.
New England 17/1/45.
Grantham 25/6/45.
Doncaster 8/9/63.

RENUMBERED:
3932 11/9/46.
63932 7/6/49.

CONDEMNED:
22/9/63.
Sold for scrap to Bulwell Forest Wagon Works.

3488

Doncaster 1575.

To traffic 3/11/23.

REPAIRS:
Don. 3/12/25-6/3/26.**G.**
Don. 14/12/27-8/3/28.**G.**
Don. 1/2-8/3/30.**G.**
Don. 23/7-27/8/32.**G.**
Don. 28/7-25/8/34.**G.**
Don. 18/7-15/8/36.**G.**
Don. 17/8-1/10/38.**G.**
Don. 27/7-31/8/40.**G.**
Don. 12/9-10/10/42.**G.**
Don. 12-19/12/42.**L.**
Don. 7/10-4/11/44.**G.**
Don. 27/4-1/6/46.**G.**
Don. 17/7-23/8/48.**G.**
Don. 18/1-14/2/51.**G.**
Don. 28/4-22/5/53.**G.**
Don. 6/3-4/4/55.**G.**
Don. 9/10-2/11/56.**C/L.**
Don. 22/12/57-25/1/58.**G.**
Don. 4/1-10/2/61.**G.**

BOILERS:
7689.
7711 *(ex3497)* 27/8/32.
8186 *(ex3471)* 1/10/38.
7707 *(ex3473)* 31/8/40.
9015 *(ex2435)* 10/10/42.
4406 *(ex2437)* 4/11/44.
21014 *(ex3491)* 14/2/51.
21067 *(ex3931)* 22/5/53.
21010 *(ex3958)* 4/4/55.
28561 *(ex1047)* 25/1/58.

SHEDS:
New England.
Doncaster 7/9/43.
Colwick 23/1/44.
New England 17/1/45.
Grantham 25/6/45.
New England 9/7/50.
Grantham 29/10/50.
New England 16/9/51.
Grantham 28/10/51.

RENUMBERED:
3933 1/6/46.
63933 21/8/48.

CONDEMNED:
29/12/62.
Sold for scrap to Central Wagon Co.Ince.

3489

Doncaster 1576.

To traffic 14/11/23.

REPAIRS:
Don. 26/10/25-23/1/26.**G.** To
3489 on 30/3/25.
Don. 29/1-19/2/26.**L.**
Don. 14/12/27-10/3/28.**G.**
Don. 15/2-15/3/30.**G.**
Don. 2/4-7/5/32.**G.**
Don. 26/5-23/6/34.**G.**
Don. 16/5-13/6/36.**G.**
Don. 4/6-2/7/38.**G.**
Don. 2/12/39-3/2/40.**G.**
Don. 18/10-22/11/41.**G.**
Don. 9/10-6/11/43.**G.**
Don. 9/2-16/3/46.**G.**
Don. 4/7-3/8/48.**G.**
Don. 15-23/3/49.**C/L.**
Don. 15/2-14/3/51.**G.**
Don. 2-30/10/53.**G.**
Don. 23/2-29/3/56.**G.**
Don. 17/12/57-9/1/58.**C/L.**
Don. 23/1-28/2/59.**G.**
Don. 8-17/7/59.**N/C.**
Don. 5-11/8/59.**N/C.**

BOILERS:
7690.
7688 *(ex3487)* 7/5/32.
8857 *(ex3457)* 2/7/38.
9247 *(new)* 22/11/41.
8973 *(ex3483)* 16/3/46.
21016 *(ex3933)* 14/3/51.
21009 *(ex3986)* 30/10/53.
21029 *(ex3973)* 29/3/56.
21069 *(ex3940)* 28/2/59.

SHEDS:
New England.
Doncaster 6/9/43.
Colwick 23/1/44.
New England 21/9/44.
Grantham 25/6/45.
Frodingham 9/2/47.
Doncaster 13/6/54.
Retford 16/10/60.

RENUMBERED:
3934 14/3/46.
63934 31/7/48.

CONDEMNED:
16/7/62.
Cut up at Doncaster.

WORKS CODES:- Cow - Cowlairs. Dar - Darlington. Don - Doncaster. Ghd - Gateshead. Gor - Gorton. Inv - Inverurie. Str - Stratford.

REPAIR CODES:- **C/H** - Casual Heavy. **C/L** - Casual Light. **G** - General. **H** - Heavy. **H/I** - Heavy Intermediate. **L** - Light. **L/I** - Light Intermediate. **N/C** - Non-Classified.

The four which Doncaster turned out in 1934, numbered 2434 to 2437 did have the benefit of newly built tender, and by then flush side panels had been adopted as the norm for 4200 gallon Group Standard tenders; they were however still Part 3. *L.N.E.R.*

Under the wartime Railway Executive Committee's authority, Doncaster were allowed to build 25 more O2 class engines, but the tenders for them were to be taken from passenger engines then in less need of the larger Group Standard type. They were placed in Part 3, although their brake equipment was not the same as the others. *L.N.E.R.*

Only the first three nos 3833/4/5 of that wartime order got LNER on their tender. Between 3835 on 26th June and 3836 on 31st July 1942, Thompson had decided that material, and even scarcer labour, could be saved by showing only N E as the owning initials. Regarding the second-hand tenders used with them, seventeen started off with the stepped top type, as shown by 3833's photograph, and the other eight - of which 3844 was one - got the later flush sided type. They did not all stay so equipped, because on twelve, tender was changed subsequently. *L.N.E.R.*

3490

Doncaster 1577.

To traffic 30/11/23 as 490N.

REPAIRS:
Don. 21/12/25-12/3/26.**G.**
Don. 30/12/27-7/3/28.**G.**
Don. 25/1-22/2/30.**G.**
Don. 1-29/10/32.**G.**
Don. 30/6-21/7/34.**G.**
Don. 1-29/8/36.**G.**
Don. 6-27/8/38.**G.**
Don. 13-20/4/40.**L.**
Don. 13/7-17/8/40.**G.**
Don. 19/4-24/5/41.**G.**
Don. 19/6-21/8/43.**G.**
Don. 2/6-14/7/45.**G.**
Don. 11/8-1/9/45.**L.**
Don. 10/10-11/11/47.**G.**
Don. 8/7-4/8/50.**G.**
Don. 23/1-13/2/51.**C/L.**
Don. 19/8-14/11/52.**G.**
Don. 5/4-21/5/54.**G.**
Don. 5/7-5/8/55.**G.**
Don. 23/2-12/4/58.**G.**
Don. 2-12/12/59.**N/C.**
Don. 26/11/60-3/1/61.**G.**

BOILERS:
7691.
8182 (new) 29/10/32.
7712 (ex3478) 27/8/38.
7714 (ex3471) 17/8/40.
4402 (ex3474) 14/7/45.
9388 (ex3976) 11/11/47.
9466 (ex3488) 4/8/50.
21002 (ex3942) 14/11/52.
21015 (ex3978) 5/8/55.
28591 (ex1213) 12/4/58.
28956 (ex1125) 3/1/61.

SHEDS:
New England.
Mexborough 7/3/28.
New England 20/4/28.
Doncaster 6/9/43.
Colwick 23/1/44.
New England 24/9/44.
Grantham 17/5/45.
New England 20/8/50.
Grantham 29/10/50.
Mexborough 28/10/51.
Doncaster 16/11/52.
Grantham 30/12/62.

RENUMBERED:
3935 9/9/46.
63935 4/8/50.

CONDEMNED:
8/9/63.
Sold for scrap to Bulwell Forest Wagon Works.

3491

Doncaster 1578.

To traffic 5/12/23.

REPAIRS:
Don. 20/3-17/7/26.**G.**
Don. 16/2-30/3/29.**G.**
Don. 8/8-3/10/31.**G.**
Don. 4-25/11/33.**G.**
Don. 1-29/6/35.**G.**
Don. 17/7-14/8/37.**G.**
Don. 28/10-25/11/39.**G.**
Don. 24/2-13/4/40.**G.**
Don. 16/5-20/6/42.**G.**
Don. 11-25/9/43.**L.**
Don. 1-29/4/44.**G.**
Don. 21/9-12/10/46.**G.**
Don. 21/4-20/5/49.**G.**
Don. 19/12/51-15/1/52.**G.**
Don. 25/5-3/8/54.**G.**
Don. 22/3-18/4/57.**G.**
Don. 27/8-2/10/59.**G.**
Don. 4/10-5/12/61.**G.**

BOILERS:
7692.
4408 (new) 25/11/33.
8182 (ex3472) 20/6/42.
8856 (ex3475) 12/10/46.
9242 (ex3938) 20/5/49.
21046 (ex3932) 15/1/52.
21045 (ex3956) 3/8/54.
21004 (ex3956) 18/4/57.
21047 (ex3929) 2/10/59.
21003 (ex3928) 5/12/61.

SHEDS:
New England.
Grantham 25/6/45.
Retford 11/6/61.

RENUMBERED:
3936 7/10/46.
63936 20/5/49.

CONDEMNED:
22/9/63.
Sold for scrap to Bulwell Forest Wagon Works.

The first of the class, later 3461, was the only one first fitted with Ramsbottom safety valves, although from October 1926 it carried boilers fitted with 'pop' type. Because O2 used the same Diagram 2 boiler as O1 class, there were interchanges leading to some of the other 3-cylinder engines being seen with Ramsbottom type, nos 3485 and 3487 being examples.

Replacement boilers to Diagram 2 built from 1935 had handholes, with covers, instead of the washout plugs fitted previously, but by 1937 the covers were disregarded, being left off for easier access, and many were seen in service without them. 3461 is at New England.

Ever ready to do a tinkering job on anything Gresley, in October 1943 Thompson had 3479 turned out changed from a Diagram 2 boiler to one of his Diagram 100A, although only working at 180 lb instead of the 225 lb of which it was capable. For that change there was also the inconvenience and expense of providing an extension to join smokebox and boiler, as clearly seen here. For that variety, Part 4 was introduced, and the opportunity was taken to change from GN type cab to one with the two side windows. Whilst there was still a danger of being machine-gunned from enemy aircraft, the leading 'window' was filled with a steel plate instead of glass. Four others were changed similarly (3487, 2954/7, and 2437) during 1944. *L.N.E.R.*

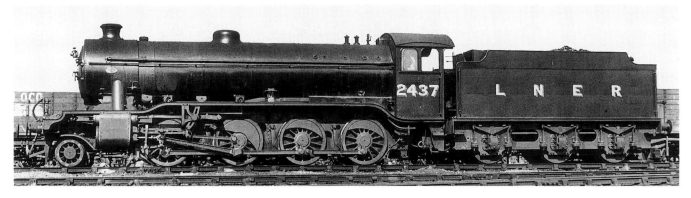

Other differences on Part 4, of which modellers need to be wary, are the anti-vacuum placed on the extension piece instead of on the smokebox, the more forward position of the dome and the safety valves, and the whistle mounted on the firebox.

3492

Doncaster 1579.

To traffic 15/12/23 as 492N.

REPAIRS:
Don. 21/12/25-17/3/26.**G.**
Don. 14/2-27/4/28.**G.**
Don. 5/7-16/8/30.**G.**
Don. 24/9-22/10/32.**G.**
Don. 31/3-5/5/34.**G.**
Don. 15/2-14/3/36.**G.**
Don. 5-31/12/36.**L.**
Don. 19/3-7/5/38.**G.**
Don. 15/6-6/7/40.**G.**
Don. 20/3-17/4/43.**G.**
Don. 19/5-23/6/45.**G.**
Don. 4/5-10/6/47.**G.**
Don. 19/11-12/12/47.**L.**
Don. 20/11-22/12/49.**G.**
Don. 3/7-1/8/52.**G.**
Don. 18-26/8/53.**N/C.**
Don. 4/12/54-7/1/55.**G.**
Don. 31/7-4/9/57.**G.**
Don. 22/8-12/10/60.**G.**

BOILERS:
7706.
7715 *(ex3501)* 22/10/32.
7709 *(ex3500)* 7/5/38.
9240 *(new)* 6/7/40.
9365 *(ex3935)* 10/6/47.
8858 *(ex3926)* 22/12/49.
21054 *(ex3939)* 1/8/52.
21061 *(ex3954)* 7/1/55.
21053 *(ex3954)* 4/9/57.
21066 *(ex3971)* 12/10/60.

SHEDS:
New England.

Doncaster 11/12/43.
Colwick 23/1/44.
New England 21/9/44.
Grantham 25/6/45.
Frodingham 9/2/47.
Retford 18/10/53.

RENUMBERED:
3937 13/9/46.
63937 22/12/49.

CONDEMNED:
8/9/63.
Sold for scrap to Bulwell Forest Wagon Works.

3493

Doncaster.

To traffic 22/12/23 as 493N.

REPAIRS:
Don. 29/3-31/7/26.**G.**
Don. 20/4-25/5/29.**G.**
Don. 7/11-12/12/31.**G.**
Don. 26/8-30/9/33.**G.** *Diamond soot blower on.*
Don. 29/6-27/7/35.**G.**
Don. 24/7-21/8/37.**G.**
Don. 6/5-24/6/39.**G.**
Don. 8-29/3/41.**G.**
Don. 17/4-15/5/43.**G.**
Don. 17/3-21/4/45.**G.**
Don. 13/5-15/6/47.**G.**
Don. 5/4-10/5/49.**G.**
Don. 12-30/8/49.**C/L.**
Don. 9/10-6/11/51.**G.**
Don. 6-27/3/53.**N/C.**
Don. 2-28/5/54.**G.**

Don. 18/1-18/2/56.**G.**
Don. 4-31/10/56.**C/L.**
Don. 6/6-16/7/58.**G.**
Don. 3/5-3/6/61.**G.**
Don. 27/11/61-20/1/62.**C/L.**

BOILERS:
7707.
7514 *(ex3485)* 30/9/33.
9242 *(new)* 29/3/41.
9240 *(ex3937)* 15/6/47.
9248 *(ex3484)* 10/5/49.
21040 *(ex3973)* 6/11/51.
21043 *(ex3960)* 28/5/54.
28148 *(ex1672)* 16/7/58.
28271 *(ex1159)* 3/6/61.

SHEDS:
New England.
Doncaster 10/12/43.
Colwick 23/1/44.
New England 24/9/44.
Grantham 25/6/45.

RENUMBERED:
3938 12/11/46.
63938 10/5/49.

CONDEMNED:
8/9/63.
Sold for scrap to Bulwell Forest Wagon Works.

3494

Doncaster 1581.

To traffic 29/12/23 as 494N.

REPAIRS:
Don. 10/2-8/6/26.**G.** *To 3494 on 30/3/25.*
Don. 25/3-28/6/28.**G.**
Don. 5/7-9/8/30.**G.**
Don. 24/12/32-4/2/33.**G.**
Don. 12/1-2/2/35.**G.**
Don. 3-17/10/36.**H.**
Don. 24/9-8/10/38.**G.**
Don. 18/5-29/6/40.**G.**
Don. 31/10-5/12/42.**G.**
Don. 16/9-7/10/44.**G.**
Don. 28/9-19/10/46.**G.**
Don. 11/7-11/8/49.**G.**
Don. 25/1-22/2/52.**G.**
Don. 2/6-9/7/54.**G.**
Don. 5/2-13/3/56.**C/L.**
Don. 14/5-20/6/57.**G.**
Don. 28/11/60-11/1/61.**G.**

BOILERS:
7708.
7501 *(ex3477)* 9/8/30.
8457 *(ex2955)* 17/10/36.
7523 *(ex3472)* 8/10/38.
9239 *(new)* 29/6/40.
8820 *(ex3479)* 7/10/44.
9244 *(ex3941)* 11/8/49.
21048 *(ex3477)* 22/2/52.
21022 *(ex3929)* 9/7/54.
21028 *(ex3961)* 20/6/57.
21040 *(ex3972)* 11/1/61.

SHEDS:
New England.
Doncaster 10/12/43.
Colwick 23/1/44.
New England 17/1/45.
Grantham 25/6/45.
Frodingham 9/2/47.
Doncaster 29/8/54.

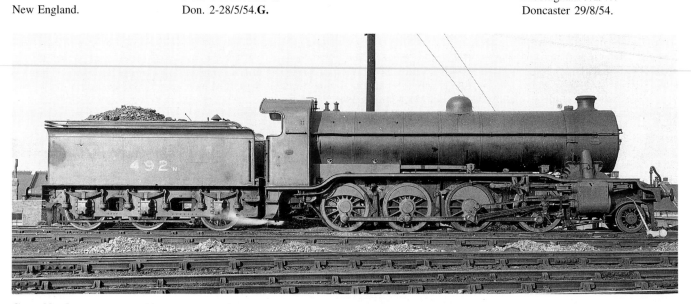

Great Northern custom had been to mount the whistle above the cab roof, and that gave a height from rail of 13' 3³/₈", so to comply with the LNER Composite Load Gauge, beginning with engine 487N, the LNER-built engines had their whistle mounted on the front of the cab, to bring its height below the required 13' 0". *N.H.Willoughby.*

In the run-up to a probable war, in early 1939 it was realised that the ten nos 3477 to 3486 were still to the GN gauge, which would inhibit any wider usage of them, so between 3485 in June 1939 and 3480 in October 1940, they were brought within the 13' 0" gauge, and the chance was taken to improve their cab to the side window type. On that type of cab the whistle was mounted on the front, but note that it was not on the centre line, being offset to the near side. *L.N.E.R.*

Retford 31/1/60.

RENUMBERED:
3939 19/10/46.
63939 11/8/49.

CONDEMNED:
22/9/63.
Sold for scrap to Bulwell Forest Wagon Works.

3495

Doncaster 1582.

To traffic 6/2/24 as 495N.

REPAIRS:
Don. 15/4-15/10/26.**G.**
Don. 18/10-28/12/28.**G.**
Don. 22/11-31/12/30.**G.**
Don. 17/6-22/7/33.**G.**
Don. 18/5-15/6/35.**G.**
Don. 17/7-7/8/37.**G.**
Don. 8-15/1/38.**G.**
Don. 27/1-2/3/40.**G.**
Don. 8/2-8/3/41.**L.**
Don. 16/5-13/6/42.**G.**
Don. 30/9-21/10/44.**G.**
Don. 1-8/9/45.**L.**
Don. 24/12/46-6/2/47.**G.**
Don. 12/4-7/5/48.**H.**
Don. 10-25/8/48.**L.**
Don. 15/8-23/9/49.**G.**
Don. 19/5-12/6/52.**G.**
Don. 5/8-1/9/54.**G.**

Don. 10/10-10/11/56.**G.**
Don. 30/12/58-3/2/59.**G.**
Don. 11-25/10/60.**N/C.**
Don. 10/7-30/8/62.**G.**

BOILERS:
7709.
7691 *(ex3490)* 22/7/33.
G982 *(ex3460)* 7/8/37.
4404 *(ex2434)* 15/1/38.
9162 *(new)* 2/3/40.
9239 *(ex3494)* 21/10/44.
9471 *(new)* 6/2/47.
9463 *(ex3930)* 7/5/48.
9015 *(ex3927)* 23/9/49.
21051 *(ex3936)* 12/6/52.
21069 *(ex3967)* 1/11/56.
21039 *(ex3987)* 3/2/59.
21020 *(ex3975)* 30/8/62.

SHEDS:
New England.
Doncaster 10/12/43.
Colwick 23/1/44.
New England 17/1/45.
Grantham 25/6/45.
Doncaster 8/9/63.

RENUMBERED:
3940 8/12/46.
63940 7/5/48.

CONDEMNED:
22/9/63.
Cut up at Doncaster.

3496

Doncaster 1584.

To traffic 23/2/24.

REPAIRS:
Don. 6/8-27/11/26.**G.**
Don. 8/12/28-9/2/29.**G.**
Don. 25/4-6/6/31.**G.**
Don. 7-28/5/32.**L.**
Don. 14/10-18/11/33.**G.**
Don. 20/7-17/8/35.**G.**
Don. 7-28/8/37.**G.**
Don. 26/8-7/10/39.**G.**
Don. 2/8-6/9/41.**G.**
Don. 13/11-4/12/43.**G.**
Don. 17/8-7/9/46.**G.**
Don. 10-23/11/48.**G.**
Don. 22/7-17/8/51.**G.**
Don. 15/3-13/4/55.**G.**
Don. 15/3-11/4/56.**C/L.**
Don. 7/1-9/2/61.**G.**

BOILERS:
7710.
7509 *(ex3480)* 18/11/33.
8457 *(ex3494)* 7/10/39.
9244 *(new)* 6/9/41.
9321 *(ex3970)* 23/11/48.
21032 *(ex3922)* 17/8/51.
21067 *(ex3933)* 13/4/55.
21054 *(ex3976)* 9/2/61.

SHEDS:
Doncaster.
New England 1/1/25.

Grantham 25/6/45.
Frodingham 9/2/47.
Langwith 12/3/50.
Doncaster 25/6/50.
Grantham 26/11/61.

RENUMBERED:
3941 7/10/46.
63941 23/11/48.

CONDEMNED:
3/9/63.
Sold for scrap to Bulwell Forest Wagon Works.

3497

Doncaster 1587.

To traffic 22/3/24.

REPAIRS:
Don. 4/1-2/4/27.**G.**
Don. 22/6-27/7/29.**G.**
Don. 26/3-30/4/32.**G.**
Don. 26/5-23/6/34.**G.**
Don. 11/4-9/5/36.**G.**
Don. 6-20/3/37.**L.**
Don. 25/6-2/7/38.**G.**
Don. 18/5-8/6/40.**G.**
Don. 19-26/4/41.**L.**
Don. 19/9-17/10/42.**G.**
Don. 24/6-29/7/44.**G.**
Don. 17/8-21/9/46.**G.**
Don. 11/4-19/5/48.**G.**
Don. 20/9-23/10/50.**G.**

WORKS CODES:- Cow - Cowlairs. Dar - Darlington. Don - Doncaster. Ghd - Gateshead. Gor - Gorton. Inv - Inverurie. Str - Stratford.

REPAIR CODES:- **C/H** - Casual Heavy. **C/L** - Casual Light. **G** - General. **H** - Heavy. **H/I** - Heavy Intermediate. **L** - Light. **L/I** - Light Intermediate. **N/C** - Non-Classified.

37

Only seven months after it was new, no.3500 went into works, and when returned to traffic on 28th January 1925, it had been fitted with this 'Dabeg' feed water heater and pump. Its exhaust steam injector under the left hand side of the cab had also been replaced by a live steam type on the firebox backplate. That system had worked successfully but was removed when it went into works for repair in October 1942, under a Thompson edict (with more justification than many of his others) issued in June 1941 to "remove all gadgets etc. at the next shopping". It can also be seen that the engines built to 1924 had their boiler handrails curved round to end on the front of the smokebox, and no doorstop was fitted.

Don. 10/9-13/10/52.**G.**
Don. 6/2-9/3/57.**H/I.**
Don. 20/3-22/4/61.**G.**
Don. 26/2-2/6/62.**C/H.**

BOILERS:
7711.
7515 *(ex3464)* 30/4/32.
8859 *(new)* 9/5/36.
7716 *(ex spare and 3463)* 17/10/42.
8857 *(ex3467)* 21/9/46.
21002 *(ex3982)* 23/10/50.
21059 *(ex3963)* 13/10/52.
21070 *(ex3968)* 22/4/61.

SHEDS:
New England.
Doncaster 10/2/43.
Colwick 23/1/44.
New England 24/9/44.
Doncaster 30/11/45.
Langwith 27/10/46.
Doncaster 25/6/50.
Retford 31/1/60.
Grantham 26/11/61.

RENUMBERED:
3942 28/7/46.
63942 19/5/48.

CONDEMNED:
8/9/63.
Cut up at Doncaster.

3498

Doncaster 1589.

To traffic 29/3/24.

REPAIRS:
Don. 9/8-11/12/26.**G.**
Don. 19/1-2/3/29.**G.**
Don. 25/4-30/5/31.**G.**
Don. 7/10-4/11/33.**G.**
Don. 13/7-10/8/35.**G.**
Don. 7-28/8/37.**G.**
Don. 9/10/37.**L.**
Don. 28/10-25/11/39.**G.**
Don. 2-9/12/39.**L.**
Don. 20/7-31/8/40.**L.**
Don. 9/11-28/12/40.**G.**
Don. 29/3-19/4/41.**L.**
Don. 31/10-26/12/42.**G.**
Don. 9/12/44-6/1/45.**G.**
Don. 20/7-17/8/46.**G.**
Don. 22/5-24/6/48.**G.**
Don. 24/8-29/9/50.**G.**
Don. 20/1-29/2/52.**C/H.**
Don. 19/1-23/2/54.**G.**
Don. 26/4-1/6/57.**G.**
Don. 7-22/2/61.**N/C.**
Don. 13/4-26/5/62.**G.**
Don. 19-29/3/63.**C/L.**

BOILERS:
7712.
8185 *(new)* 4/11/33.

7691 *(ex3495)* 28/8/37.
8859 *(ex3497)* 26/12/42.
8976 *(ex3467)* 17/8/46.
8821 *(ex3921)* 24/6/48.
21001 *(ex3964)* 29/9/50.
21018 *(ex3983)* 23/2/54.
21045 *(ex3936)* 1/6/57.
21061 *(ex3962)* 26/5/62.

SHEDS:
New England.
Doncaster 12/12/43.
Colwick 23/1/44.
New England 24/9/44.
Doncaster 20/11/45.
Langwith 27/10/46.
Doncaster 25/6/50.
Grantham 27/11/60.
Retford 11/6/61.
Grantham 16/7/61.
Doncaster 8/9/63.

RENUMBERED:
3943 17/8/46.
63943 24/6/48.

CONDEMNED:
22/9/63.
Cut up at Doncaster.

3499

Doncaster 1592.

To traffic 26/4/24.

REPAIRS:
Don. 13/3-5/4/25.**L.**
Don. 4/12/26-12/3/27.**G.**
Don. 9/2-23/3/29.**G.**
Don. 4/7-15/8/31.**G.** *Gresham F.W.heater.*
Don. 4/11-9/12/33.**G.**
Don. 3/8-7/9/35.**G.**
Don. 25/9-16/10/37.**G.** *F.W.H.removed.*
Don. 16/12/39-27/1/40.**G.**
Don. 6/12/41-17/1/42.**G.**
Don. 8/1-12/2/44.**G.**
Don. 30/5-11/7/47.**G.**
Don. 12-31/3/48.**L.**
Don. 31/1-11/3/49.**G.**
Don. 3/9-5/10/51.**G.**
Don. 20/12/51-7/1/52.**N/C.**
Don. 9/5-4/6/54.**G.**
Don. 16/7-23/8/56.**G.**
Don. 12/3-24/4/59.**G.**
Don. 14-23/12/60.**N/C.**
Don. 27/3-3/4/61.*Not repaired.*

BOILERS:
7713.
8184 *(new)* 9/12/33.
8972 *(ex2954)* 27/1/40.
8456 *(ex3489)* 11/3/49.
21035 *(ex3480)* 5/10/51.
21012 *(ex3967)* 4/6/54.

SHEDS:
New England.
Doncaster 30/11/45.
Frodingham 20/10/47.
Doncaster 13/6/54.
Retford 10/2/57.

RENUMBERED:
3944 2/6/46.
63944 31/3/48.

CONDEMNED:
3/4/61.
Cut up at Doncaster.

3500

Doncaster 1594.

To traffic 22/5/24.

REPAIRS:
Don. 20/12/24-28/1/25.**L.**
Dabeg F.W.H.fitted.
Don. 15/7-26/9/25.**L.**

By 1931 a stop to limit the swing of the smokebox door was being fitted between the hinges, and then from 1932, the boiler handrails began to be cut back to end on the side instead of on the front of the smokebox. Progress on that handrail alteration was slow, because when ex works in May 1947, no.3931 (ex 3486) still had curved ends. It was probably the last, because none were seen with them in B.R.numbering. *E.V.Fry.*

Don. 31/1-21/5/27.**G.**
Don. 4/5-8/6/29.**G.**
Don. 1-29/8/31.**G.**
Don. 4/11-9/12/33.**G.**
Don. 14/12/35-18/1/36.**G.**
Don. 5-26/2/38.**G.**
Don. 15/6-13/7/40.**G.**
Don. 17/10-5/12/42.**G.** *Dabeg F.W.H.removed.*
Don. 2/12/44-6/1/45.**G.**
Don. 21-24/1/45.**N/C.**
Don. 26/10-4/12/46.**G.**
Don. 12/9-25/10/48.**G.**
Don. 4/4-8/5/50.**G.**
Don. 5-30/5/52.**G.**
Don. 10/9-9/10/52.**C/L.**
Don. 28/7-20/8/54.**G.**
Don. 10/10/-23/11/56.**G.**
Don. 9/7-7/8/59.**G.**
Don. 9/2-15/3/62.**G.**
Don. 19-30/3/62.**N/C.**

BOILERS:
7714.
7709 *(ex3495)* 9/12/33.
7717 *(ex3470)* 26/2/38.
9014 *(ex2436)* 5/12/42.
8855 *(ex3953)* 25/10/48.
9471 *(ex3478)* 8/5/50.
21050 *(ex3485)* 30/5/52.
21026 *(ex3984)* 20/8/54.
28500 *(ex1616)* 23/11/56.
28959 *(new)* 7/8/59.

SHEDS:
New England.
Doncaster 30/11/45.
Langwith 15/12/46.
Doncaster 25/6/50.
Frodingham 12/4/53.
Retford 3/1/54.

RENUMBERED:
3945 5/9/46.
63945 23/10/48.

CONDEMNED:
22/9/63.
Sold for scrap to Bulwell Forest Wagon Works.

3501

Doncaster 1595.

To traffic 7/6/24.

REPAIRS:
Don. 15/5-20/6/25.**L.**
Don. 18/8-1/11/27.**G.**
Don. 17/1-24/2/28.**L.**
Don. 16/11-14/12/29.**G.**
Don. 23/4-28/5/32.**G.**
Don. 14/7-25/8/34.**G.**
Don. 13/6-4/7/36.**G.**
Don. 2-23/7/38.**G.**
Don. 14/9-26/10/40.**G.**
Don. 20/2-20/3/43.**G.**
Don. 25/11-25/12/44.**G.**
Don. 2-30/3/46.**G.**
Don. 17/1-13/2/48.**G.**
Don. 5/4-9/5/49.**C/H.**
Don. 15/7-3/8/49.**C/L.**
Don. 26/9-24/10/50.**G.**
Don. 18/6-25/7/52.**G.**
Don. 25/10-23/11/54.**G.**
Don. 6/11-5/12/57.**G.**
Don. 26/1-14/2/59.**C/L.**
Don. 19/8-1/10/60.**G.**

BOILERS:
7715.
7719 *(ex3470)* 28/5/32.
7510 *(ex3476)* 23/7/38.
9245 *(new)* 26/10/40.
8459 *(ex3882)* 13/2/48.
9014 *(ex3945)* 9/5/49.
21003 *(ex3937)* 24/10/50.
21053 *(ex3948)* 25/7/52.

21052 *(ex3961)* 23/11/54.
21044 *(ex3953)* 5/12/57.
21004 *(ex3936)* 1/10/60.

SHEDS:
Newport.
New England 28/2/25.
Doncaster 11/12/45.
Langwith 27/10/46.
Doncaster 25/6/50.
Grantham 5/4/53.
Retford 16/7/61.

RENUMBERED:
3946 30/3/46.
E3946 13/2/48.
63946 9/5/49.

CONDEMNED:
7/4/63.
Cut up at Doncaster.

2954

Doncaster 1773.

To traffic 23/4/32.

REPAIRS:
Str. 21/5-6/7/33.**H.**
Don. 24/7-4/9/34.**G.**
Don. 8/6-15/8/36.**G.**
Don. 15/8-6/9/37.**G.**
Don. 18/3-29/4/39.**G.**
Don. 19/10-16/11/40.**G.**
Don. 27/6-8/8/42.**G.**
Don. 29/7-26/8/44.**G.**
Don. 18/5-22/6/46.**G.**
Don. 30/5-27/6/47.**L.**
Don. 5/4-11/5/48.**G.**
Don. 7/5-9/6/50.**G.**
Don. 13/5-3/7/53.**G.**
Don. 30/4-29/5/56.**C/L.**

Don. 9/12/57-18/1/58.**G.**
Don. 27/2-4/3/59.**C/L.**
Don. 27/2-14/4/60.**C/L.**
Don. 28/4/61.*Not repaired.*

BOILERS:
8456.
8974 *(new)* 15/8/36.
8972 *(ex2955)* 6/9/37.
4401 *(ex2437)* 29/4/39.
9440 *(new)* 26/8/44.
9394 *(ex3972)* 9/6/50.
21017 *(ex3966)* 3/7/53.

SHEDS:
March.
Doncaster 25/6/50.
Retford 23/2/58.

RENUMBERED:
3947 1/12/46.
63947 8/5/48.

CONDEMNED:
28/4/61.
Cut up at Doncaster.

2955

Doncaster 1774.

To traffic 19/5/32.

REPAIRS:
Don. 19/7-9/9/33.**G.**
Don. 23/6-4/8/34.**G.**
Don. 3/5-25/7/36.**G.**
Don. 1-28/8/37.**G.**
Don. 15/4-20/5/39.**G.**
Don. 18/1-15/2/41.**G.**
Don. 24/10/42-2/1/43.**G.**
Don. 23/9-21/10/44.**G.**
Don. 21/7-25/8/45.**G.**

Don. 31/8-15/10/47.**G.**
Don. 11/12/48-5/1/49.**L.**
Don. 1/1-4/2/50.**G.**
Don. 30/3-30/4/52.**G.**
Don. 20-30/7/53.**C/L.**
Don. 11/8-24/9/53.**C/L.**
Don. 3-15/6/54.**C/L.**
Don. 3/9-9/10/54.**G.**
Don. 5/12/56-12/1/57.**G.**
Don. 29/7-28/8/59.**G.**

BOILERS:
8457.
8972 *(new)* 25/7/36.
8462 *(ex2960)* 28/8/37.
8974 *(ex2960)* 2/1/43.
9164 *(ex3461)* 15/10/47
9317 *(ex3966)* 4/2/50.
21049 *(ex3955)* 30/4/52.
21035 *(ex3944)* 9/10/54.
21051 *(ex3940)* 12/1/57.
28962 *(new)* 28/8/59.

SHEDS:
March.
Grantham 14/5/50.
New England 9/7/50.
Grantham 14/1/51.

RENUMBERED:
3948 15/12/46.
63948 5/1/49.

CONDEMNED:
16/10/62.
Sold for scrap to Central Wagon Co.Ince.

The smokebox door was fitted with a short cross rail just above the top hinge strap, and the top lamp iron was on the door. Even when the British Railways cast number plate was introduced, there was no necessity to move the rail or to put the lamp iron higher. Note the addition of the oval shed allocation plate on the door. *E.Haigh.*

(right centre) **In later years there were some deviations to be seen on smokebox doors as a result of exchanges. In 1963, its final year, 63984 had a door with shorter rail mounted above the number plate, and with the door knob further away from the rim than was usual. Other items to note are that it has been fitted with complete Automatic Warning System, and has guard irons only on its pony truck, although when new it had also had the longer irons fixed on the end of the frame and known not needed.** *M.S.Eggenton.*

(right) **Door stop variation persisted through to withdrawal of the class. Whilst no.63984 has a single one between the hinges, 63974 still has the type on which the hinge straps were extended to form stops, and also has original rail and door knob position. Ex works 28th April 1962, by 13th May, when this photograph was taken, it had suffered a mishap, but insufficient for a further works visit.**

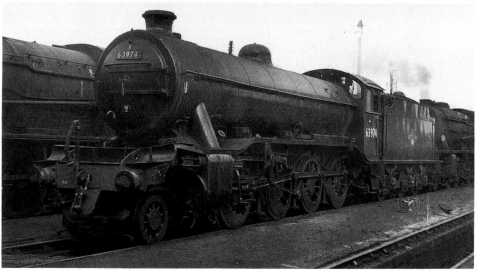

2956

Doncaster 1775.

To traffic 28/5/32.

REPAIRS:
Str. 9/2-24/3/33.**H.**
Don. 4/6-4/8/34.**G.**
Don. 10/5-10/7/36.**G.**
Don. 29/8-2/10/37.**G.**
Don. 25/3-13/5/39.**G.**
Don. 23/11/40-1/1/41.**G.**
Don. 7/2-28/3/42.**L.**
Don. 19/12/42-16/1/43.**G.**
Don. 11/11-9/12/44.**G.**
Don. 1/3-22/5/47.**G.**
Don. 3-26/5/49.**G.**
Don. 23/3-23/4/51.**G.**
Don. 19/5-13/7/53.**G.**
Don. 27/7-31/8/55.**G.**
Don. 4/7-6/8/58.**G.**
Don. 7/3-15/4/61.**G.**

BOILERS:
8458.
8459 *(ex2957)* 10/7/36.
9012 *(new)* 2/10/37.
9364 *(new)* 16/1/43.

9318 *(ex3967)* 26/5/49.
21020 *(ex3958)* 23/4/51.
21068 *(ex3947)* 13/7/53.
28199 *(ex1077)* 31/8/55.
28129 *(ex1638)* 6/8/58.
28819 *(ex3950)* 15/4/61.

SHEDS:
March.
Grantham 4/6/50.
New England 16/9/51.
Mexborough 28/10/51.
Retford 17/8/52.
Grantham 26/11/61.

RENUMBERED:
3949 17/3/46.
63949 26/5/49.

CONDEMNED:
8/9/63.
Cut up at Doncaster.

2957

Doncaster 1776.

To traffic 23/6/32.

REPAIRS:
Str. 16/6-27/7/33.**H.**
Don. 11/7-27/8/34.**G.**
Don. 23/3-16/5/36.**G.**
Don. 24/7-20/8/37.**G.**
Don. 11/2-11/3/39.**G.**
Don. 27/7-7/9/40.**G.**
Don. 29/8-3/10/42.**G.**
Don. 3/6-15/7/44.**G.**
Don. 4-25/11/44.**L.**
Don. 28/3-21/5/47.**G.**
Don. 5/6-21/7/49.**G.**
Don. 29/5-5/7/51.**G.**
Don. 12/10-7/11/53.**G.**
Don. 17/8-24/9/55.**G.**
Don. 26/9-1/10/55.**N/C.**
Don. 9/8-21/9/57.**G.**

BOILERS:
8459.
8858 *(new)* 16/5/36.
7719 *(ex3501)* 11/3/39.
9438 *(new)* 15/7/44.
9760 *(ex1174)* 21/7/49.
28150 *(ex1174)* 5/7/51.
28356 *(ex1281)* 7/11/53.
28819 *(ex1636)* 21/9/57.

SHEDS:
March.
Grantham 14/5/50.
New England 16/9/51.
Grantham 28/10/51.

RENUMBERED:
3950 15/12/46.
63950 21/7/49.

CONDEMNED:
8/11/60.
Cut up at Doncaster.

2958

Doncaster 1777.

To traffic 7/7/32.

REPAIRS:
Don. 18/9-31/10/34.**G.**
Don. 18/7-2/10/36.**G.**
Don. 30/9-29/10/37.**G.**
Don. 4/2-4/3/39.**G.**
Don. 9/11-7/12/40.**G.**
Don. 17/10-21/11/42.**G.**
Don. 23/9-14/10/44.**G.**

3481 shows minor detail changes which began to be effective in the early 1930's. The redundant extra lamp iron which had been used in Great Northern days for codes applicable only in the London area, had been removed, and on this engine the load class collar had been taken off the vacuum standpipe. This illustration also shows the Spencer double case buffers, which were fitted on all except no.3461 which had the GN parallel shank type. None were changed to Group Standard type buffers. *W.L.Good.*

The first 26 engines were coupled with the GN class B tender, and on that type the rear buffers were the normal parallel case with circular flange type. This May 1963 photograph shows the battery box fitted under the cab for the electrical operation of the Automatic Warning System, and the tender is carrying tablet exchange apparatus of Whittaker type for use on the single line High Dyke branch. Five Grantham shedded engines were so fitted on both sides of their tender to work iron ore trains from that branch; they were nos 63929-32/40.

Don. 28/4-9/6/45.**L.**	**2959**	21065 (ex3932) 7/5/58.
Don. 24/2-4/4/47.**G.**		
Don. 2/9-17/11/47.**H.**	Doncaster 1778.	*SHEDS:*
Don. 10/7-12/8/49.**G.**		March.
Don. 19/6-24/7/51.**G.**	To traffic 11/7/32.	Doncaster 21/5/50.
Don. 22/10-21/11/53.**G.**		
Don. 24/12/55-28/1/56.**G.**	*REPAIRS:*	*RENUMBERED:*
Don. 29/7-2/9/58.**G.**	Don. 3/8-3/9/34.**G.**	**3952** 5/1/47.
Don. 12/6/62.*Not repaired.*	Don. 21/6-31/8/36.**G.**	**63952** 11/2/49.
	Don. 31/8-2/10/37.**G.**	
BOILERS:	Don. 24/6-29/7/39.**G.**	*CONDEMNED:*
8460.	Don. 19/4-24/5/41.**G.**	27/4/61.
8458 (ex2956) 2/10/36.	Don. 20/2-27/3/43.**G.**	*Cut up at Doncaster.*
4408 (ex3491) 21/11/42.	Don. 23/12/44-27/1/45.**G.**	
9470 (ex3974) 12/8/49.	Don. 24/2-1/4/47.**G.**	
21029 (ex3952) 24/7/51.	Don. 5-26/9/47.**L.**	**2960**
21007 (ex3484) 21/11/53.	Don. 17/1-11/2/49.**G.**	
21020 (ex3958) 28/1/56.	Don. 7/3-9/4/49.**C/H.**	Doncaster 1779.
21007 (ex3973) 2/9/58.	Don. 1-29/5/51.**G.**	
	Don. 21/7-13/8/51.**C/L.**	To traffic 29/7/32.
SHEDS:	Don. 3/11-16/12/52.**C/L.**	
March.	Don. 3/10-4/11/53.**G.**	*REPAIRS:*
Doncaster 21/5/50.	Don. 18/11-19/12/55.**G.**	Don. 20/8-29/9/34.**G.**
Retford 16/10/60.	Don. 27/3-7/5/58.**G.**	Don. 5/7-17/9/36.**G.**
	Don. 16/8-2/9/58.**C/L.**	Don. 29/8-1/10/37.**G.**
RENUMBERED:	Don. 7-20/8/59.**C/L.**	Don. 18/2-18/3/39.**G.**
3951 17/3/46.	Don. 19/9-6/10/59.**N/C.**	Don. 28/9-2/11/40.**G.**
63951 12/8/49.	Don. 27/4/61.*Not repaired.*	Don. 3/10-7/11/42.**G.**
		Don. 5-26/8/44.**G.**
CONDEMNED:	*BOILERS:*	Don. 19/10-15/11/46.**G.**
25/6/62.	8461.	Don. 31/8-2/10/47.**L.**
Cut up at Doncaster.	8975 (new) 31/8/36.	Don. 16/5-10/6/49.**G.**
	9013 (new) 2/10/37.	Don. 16/10-28/11/50.**G.**
	9366 (new) 27/3/43.	Don. 21/10-17/11/52.**G.**
	9163 (ex3478) 11/2/49.	Don. 14/2-15/3/55.**G.**
	21024 (ex3929) 29/5/51.	Don. 3/10-2/11/57.**G.**
	21070 (ex3976) 4/11/53.	Don. 12/2-4/3/59.**C/L.**

BOILERS:
8462.
8976 (new) 17/9/36.
8974 (ex2954) 1/10/37.
8855 (ex3465) 7/11/42.
9387 (ex3845) 15/11/46.
9361 (ex3483) 10/6/49.
21008 (ex spare) 28/11/50.
21010 (ex3954) 17/11/52.
21044 (ex3932) 15/3/55.
21034 (ex3981) 2/11/57.

SHEDS:
March.
Doncaster 21/5/50.

RENUMBERED:
3953 17/3/46.
63953 10/6/49.

CONDEMNED:
8/11/60.
Cut up at Doncaster.

2961

Doncaster 1780.

To traffic 17/8/32.

REPAIRS:
Don. 11/1-7/4/34.**G.**
Don. 16/3-4/5/35.**G.**
Don. 28/9-11/11/36.**G.**
Don. 3/10-3/11/37.**G.**
Don. 26/11-24/12/38.**L.**
Don. 22/7-2/9/39.**G.**
Don. 7/6-12/7/41.**G.**
Don. 13/3-3/4/43.**G.**
Don. 3/2-17/3/45.**G.**
Don. 25/5-13/7/46.**G.**
Don. 16/2-16/3/47.**L.**
Don. 29/4-8/7/47.**L.**
Don. 26/4-28/5/48.**G.**
Dar. 3/12/49-11/1/50.**C/L.**
Don. 14/11-14/12/50.**G.**
Don. 6-31/10/52.**G.**
Don. 19/11-17/12/54.**G.**
Don. 21/6-27/7/57.**G.**

BOILERS:
8463.
8456 (ex2954) 11/11/36.
8459 (ex2956) 3/11/37.
8858 (ex2957) 2/9/39.
9466 (new) 17/3/45.
9469 (ex3958) 28/5/48.
21010 (ex3953) 14/12/50.
21061 (ex3970) 31/10/52.
21053 (ex3946) 17/12/54.
21022 (ex3939) 27/7/57.

It was 1952 before action was taken to remove the long guard irons fitted on the end of the frame, although it had been known for twenty years that they were not really needed, the short ones on the pony truck being sufficiently effective. But 63964 here in July 1953 missed out on removal when ex works the previous March, so would not be brought into line until its June 1955 general repair. *E.V.Fry.*

SHEDS:
March.
Doncaster 21/5/50.
Retford 31/1/60.

RENUMBERED:
3954 24/12/46.
63954 28/5/48.

CONDEMNED:
14/3/61.
Cut up at Doncaster.

2430

Doncaster 1781.

To traffic 29/11/33.

REPAIRS:
Don. 18/7-21/8/35.**G.**
Don. 9/5-1/7/37.**G.**
Don. 12/11-10/12/38.**G.**
Don. 18/11/39-13/1/40.**G.**
Don. 22/11/41-3/1/42.**G.**
Don. 21/8-2/10/43.**G.**
Don. 28/4-26/5/45.**L.**
Don. 20/4-25/5/46.**G.**
Don. 7-28/11/46.**L.**
Don. 3/5-7/6/48.**G.**
Don. 31/1-16/3/50.**G.**

Don. 3/9-16/10/51.**G.**
Don. 14/9-9/10/53.**G.**
Don. 18/10-10/11/55.**G.**
Don. 24/2-3/4/59.**G.**
Don. 26/4/62.*Not repaired.*

BOILERS:
8183.
9160 *(new)* 10/12/38.
7692 *(ex3487)* 3/1/42.
9012 *(ex2956)* 2/10/43.
9362 *(ex3457)* 25/5/46.
9399 *(ex3987)* 16/3/50.
21037 *(ex3985)* 16/10/51.
21062 *(ex3968)* 10/11/55.
28300 *(ex1669)* 3/4/59.

SHEDS:
March.
Doncaster 21/5/50.
Retford 16/10/60.

RENUMBERED:
3955 23/5/46.
63955 7/6/48.

CONDEMNED:
7/5/62.
Cut up at Doncaster.

2431

Doncaster 1782.

To traffic 8/12/33.

REPAIRS:
Don. 23/7-24/8/35.**G.**
Don. 8/2-3/4/37.**G.**
Don. 17/7-17/8/38.**G.**
Don. 18/11-23/12/39.**G.**
Don. 12/7-23/8/41.**G.**
Don. 3-31/7/43.**G.**
Don. 4-11/9/43.**L.**
Don. 26/5-7/7/45.**G.**
Don. 26/1-9/2/46.**L.**
Don. 4/9-17/10/47.**G.**
Don. 14/11-16/12/49.**G.**
Don. 23/9-6/10/50.**C/L.**
Don. 17/2-5/3/51.**C/L.**
Don. 9/12/51-8/1/52.**G.**
Don. 4/6-9/7/54.**G.**
Don. 2/1-2/2/57.**G.**
Don. 14/4-12/6/57.**C/L.**
Don. 1-2/6/60.**N/C.**
Don. 20/11-30/12/61.**G.**

BOILERS:
4406.
8456 *(ex2961)* 17/8/38.
8183 *(ex2430)* 23/12/39.
9468 *(new)* 7/7/45.

9392 *(ex3980)* 16/12/49.
Renumbered 21004 6/10/50.
21045 *(ex3960)* 8/1/52.
21004 *(ex3974)* 9/7/54.
21041 *(ex3960)* 2/2/57.
28149 *(ex1087)* 30/12/61.

SHEDS:
March.
Doncaster 21/5/50.
Grantham 27/11/60.

RENUMBERED:
3956 17/9/46.
63956 16/12/49.

CONDEMNED:
8/9/63.
Sold for scrap to Bulwell Forest Wagon Works.

2432

Doncaster 1783.

To traffic 15/12/33.

REPAIRS:
Don. 18/7-29/8/35.**G.**
Don. 25/4-11/6/37.**G.**
Don. 15/10-5/11/38.**G.**

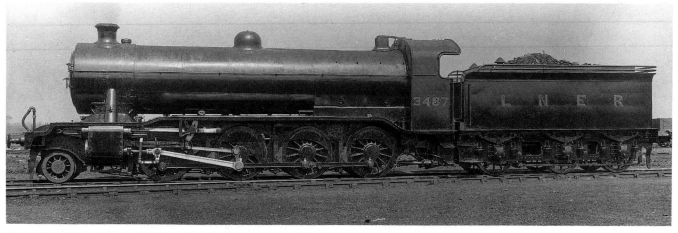

Ex works in May 1931, no.3487 had been fitted with a set of Hiduminium alloy connecting rods which were so much lighter that, in the works, each could be carried by only one man. Despite 3487 retaining them, no others were so fitted.

Don. 24/6-22/7/39.**G.**
Don. 15/2-15/3/41.**G.**
Don. 25/7-22/8/42.**G.**
Don. 3-24/6/44.**G.**
Don. 23/2-23/3/46.**G.**
Don. 26/5-25/6/48.**G.**
Don. 6/7-2/8/50.**G.**
Don. 13-22/6/51.**C/L.**
Don. 8/1-4/2/53.**G.**
Don. 22/10-26/11/55.**G.**
Don. 6/2-15/3/58.**G.**

BOILERS:
  4405.
  8460 *(ex2434)* 5/11/38.
  4405 *(ex spare)* 22/7/39.
  7710 *(ex3484)* 22/8/42.
  9462 *(ex3494)* 25/6/48.
  9385 *(ex3931)* 2/8/50.
  21063 *(ex3972)* 4/2/53.
  21037 *(ex3955)* 26/11/55.
  21000 *(ex3963)* 15/3/58.

SHEDS:
March.
Doncaster 21/5/50.
Grantham 14/6/59.

RENUMBERED:
  3957 23/3/46.
  63957 25/6/48.

CONDEMNED:
4/7/61.
Cut up at Doncaster.

2433

Doncaster 1784.

To traffic 28/12/33.

REPAIRS:
Don. 2/8-4/9/35.**G.**

Don. 29/3-22/5/37.**G.**
Don. 1-22/10/38.**G.**
Don. 30/3-27/4/40.**G.**
Don. 17/1-14/2/42.**G.**
Don. 28/8-18/9/43.**G.**
Don. 2/6-14/7/45.**G.**
Don. 1-8/12/45.**L.**
Don. 27/6-10/8/47.**G.**
Don. 24/3-30/4/48.**H.**
Don. 11/4-14/5/49.**G.**
Don. 8/2-1/3/51.**G.**
Don. 16/6-26/7/53.**G.**
Don. 17/7-15/8/55.**G.**
Don. 20/10-2/11/56.**C/L.**
Don. 23/2-29/3/58.**G.**

BOILERS:
  4407.
  9160 *(ex2430)* 14/2/42.
  9469 *(new)* 14/7/45.
  9013 *(ex3474)* 30/4/48.
  9322 *(ex3971)* 14/5/49.
  21015 *(ex3967)* 1/3/51.
  21020 *(ex3949)* 26/7/53.
  21002 *(ex3935)* 15/8/55.
  21037 *(ex3957)* 29/3/58.

SHEDS:
March.
Doncaster 25/6/50.

RENUMBERED:
  3958 16/9/46.
  63958 30/4/48.

CONDEMNED:
4/5/61.
Cut up at Doncaster.

2434

Doncaster 1785.

To traffic 20/1/34.

REPAIRS:
Don. 14/8-18/9/35.**G.**
Don. 1/6-13/7/37.**G.**
Don. 14/4-3/6/38.**G.**
Don. 6/1-17/2/40.**G.**
Don. 20/9-18/10/41.**G.**
Don. 31/7-28/8/43.**G.**
Don. 16/6-28/7/45.**G.**
Don. 9/6-15/9/47.**G.**
Don. 12-31/1/49.**L.**
Don. 14/3-21/4/49.**C/L.**
Don. 23/3-26/4/50.**G.**
Don. 17/12/52-16/1/53.**G.**
Don. 12/11-10/12/54.**G.**
Don. 25/8-28/9/57.**G.**

BOILERS:
  4404.
  8460 *(ex2958)* 13/7/37.
  8976 *(ex2960)* 3/6/38.
  8462 *(ex2955)* 28/8/43.
  4405 *(ex3477)* 26/4/50.
  21000 *(ex3476)* 16/1/53.
  21057 *(ex3982)* 10/12/54.
  21055 *(ex3982)* 28/9/57.

SHEDS:
March.
Doncaster 25/6/50.
Retford 23/2/58.

RENUMBERED:
  3959 16/9/46.
  63959 31/1/49.

CONDEMNED:
19/10/60.
Cut up at Doncaster.

2435

Doncaster 1786.

To traffic 27/1/34.

REPAIRS:
Don. 8/8-19/9/35.**G.**
Don. 13/6-24/7/37.**G.**
Don. 17/12/38-21/1/39.**G.**
Don. 3/8-14/9/40.**G.**
Don. 26/12/42-20/2/43.**G.**
Don. 18/11-16/12/44.**G.**
Don. 1/1-17/3/47.**G.**
Don. 2-24/9/47.**L.**
Don. 12/2-11/3/49.**G.**
Don. 13/11-6/12/51.**G.**
Don. 6/11-9/12/53.**C/L.**
Don. 14/4-18/5/54.**G.**
Don. 28/10-29/11/54.**C/L.**
Don. 10/12/56-16/1/57.**G.**
Don. 10/7-7/8/59.**G.**
Don. 3/10-9/12/61.**G.**

BOILERS:
  4403.
  9015 *(new)* 24/7/37.
  8456 *(ex2431)* 14/9/40.
  9363 *(new)* 20/2/43.
  9395 *(ex3983)* 11/3/49.
  21043 *(ex3938)* 6/12/51.
  21041 *(ex3979)* 18/5/54.
  21026 *(ex3945)* 16/1/57.
  28960 *(new)* 7/8/59.

SHEDS:
March.
Grantham 21/5/49.

RENUMBERED:
  3960 6/10/46.
  63960 11/3/49.

CONDEMNED:
8/9/63.
Cut up at Doncaster.

Ten of the fifteen engines in Part 2 remained as built, apart from minor changes of detail, and 63936 shows that they kept right hand drive, square corners to the buffer beam, and never had sight screens fitted on the cab side, nor did those with double window cab acquire that amenity. *K.R.Pirt.*

The class of 67 engines only had nineteen new tenders built to be coupled with them. Doncaster sent tenders to Glasgow for the ten engines from N.B.Loco.Co. and at least four of them were of the early class B type holding 5½ tons coal and 3670 gallons water. They could be identified by the equal spacing of their axles, as seen with this one, first fitted to no.477.

The early Group Standard tenders taken from J38 class, and coupled with engines 2954 to 2961 also 2430 to 2433 had vertical handrail at each end, but they were only 2' 10½" tall and no alteration was made when they were first put with 02 class. *A.G.Ellis.*

At the first general repair of 2954-61 in 1934, and of 2430-3 in 1935, the tender handrails were changed to 3' 9½", which had been made standard in December 1932. Because nos 2434-7 had new tenders built for them they had the taller rails as new. *W.L.Good.*

The 25 engines built during the war, nos 3833 to 3857 were provided with tenders taken from D49 class, seventeen with stepped top, and eight flush sided. Although changes were made, they were restricted to that group of 25, with only a couple of exceptions, two of the stepped top type being exchanged for flush sided from K3 class engines. In December 1949, no.63967 took one from 61943, and in March 1956 the one seen here with 63984 came from 61982. Note the higher backplate to the coal space, which had been fitted in March 1956. *A.G.Ellis.*

Because much of class O2's work was on the main line, from 1959, many of them were equipped with the Automatic Warning System, and with the receiver fixed on the pony truck, a sloping steel plate had to be added to protect it from damage from any swinging of the front coupling. Although coupled with one of the stepped top tenders, note it has been fitted with the higher backplate.

(opposite top) **This is one of those "Not what it seems" pictures, but fortunately I can present the true account of it. The first of the 25 wartime order, no.3833 into traffic on 22nd May 1942 was the last to do so with LNER on its tender. The next one 3834 was entered into stock on 10th June, but here on the 12th was still at the works for this picture to be taken for press propaganda purposes about a saving of steel for munitions. When it did go into traffic, it was with a Group Standard 4200 gallon tender taken from D49 class 251, and which V2 class 3657 had been using temporarily, and that tender was the first to have N E instead of L N E R. As well as advertising their saving of steel by using second-hand tenders for the 02's, there was also further saving to be publicised from the conversion of ex G.C. 0-8-0 tender engines into 0-8-0 tanks for heavy shunting work. So, one of those G.C. 4000 gallon tenders was buffered up, but not coupled, to 3834 for the press picture to be taken. In Group Standard tenders, the frame slots are parallel top and bottom; G.C. tenders had curved top to the slots.** *L.N.E.R.*

(opposite middle) **When 3835 was completed in June, it too was held back from traffic for complexion complexities. During July 1942, instead of having 3835 and N E applied by shaded transfers, it first had the figures painted on the cab without any shading to them, and in place of the 12" N E, a painted version of the L N E R totem appeared. That style was not accepted for the O2's, the rest having the usual shaded transfers, but only N E on their tender. But here was 'coming events casting their shadow before them' Doncaster <u>did</u> use that totem on the conversions it made from 0-8-0 tender to 0-8-0 tank type, but applied as a cast metal plate, and not just painted. Then, from December 1946, when stocks of shaded transfers were beginning to be exhausted, it was considered too expensive to replenish them and 12" yellow painted and unshaded figures, in the same style as 3835, replaced them.** *British Railways.*

The Automatic Warning System could involve a brake application, and to make it, air reservoirs were provided, their small cylinders being fitted under the running plate on both sides, adjacent to the rear coupled wheels. Although only one battery box was needed, it could, and was, fitted on either side of the cab. This illustration clearly shows a small detail difference peculiar to the final 25 engines, which had cut-away lower corners to their buffer beam. It also shows that from July 1956, no.63983 was one of those to change from Diagram 2 to 100A boiler, identifiable by the five handholes on the firebox for washing out purposes. *M.S.Eggenton.*

With the change to left-hand drive made from no.2954, the mechanical lubricators were mounted on the left hand running plate, and Wakefield No.7's were standardised. Although the axleboxes had mechanical, the horn cheeks had simpler lubrication, the leading three pairs having worsted trimmings. For the rear pair which were adjacent to the firebox, there was a small siphon oil box on the running plate, but starting with no.2956 in July 1936, horn cheek lubrication was centralised.

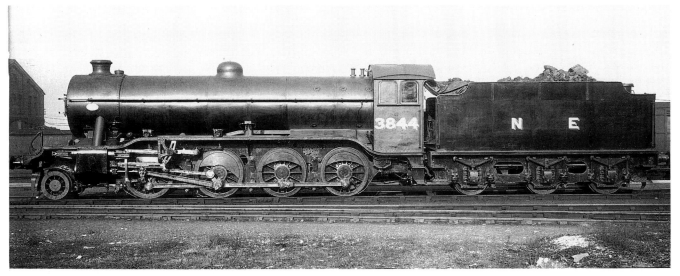

Nos 3836 to 3857 then went into traffic in the same style as 3844, which is included mainly to show two details entirely due to war conditions. The tarpaulin screen connecting cab roof and tender, was an Air Raid Precaution, so as to prevent glare when the firebox door was opened, and also in that connection the cab windows were blacked over. Later experience led to the leading one being replaced by steel sheet. This view also gives clear indication of how horn cheek lubrication was centralised using the position between the second and third coupled wheels on the running plate. *L.N.E.R.*

2436

Doncaster 1787.

To traffic 20/2/34.

REPAIRS:
Don. 16/8-25/9/35.**G.**
Don. 24/12/35-22/2/36.**L.**
Don. 11/7-14/8/37.**G.**
Don. 16/10-2/11/37.**L.**
Don. 22/4-27/5/39.**G.**
Don. 1/2-1/3/41.**G.**
Don. 29/8-19/9/42.**G.**
Don. 15/7-5/8/44.**G.**
Don. 18/5-6/7/46.**G.**
Don. 24/5-18/6/48.**G.**
Don. 10/9-4/10/49.**C/L.**
Don. 31/12/49-27/1/50.**G.**
Don. 28/5-2/7/52.**G.**
Don. 12/10-11/11/54.**G.**
Don. 2/5-14/6/57.**G.**
Don. 11/2-7/3/59.**C/H.**
Don. 23/1-23/2/60.**G.**

BOILERS:
4402.
9014 (new) 14/8/37.
8457 (ex3496) 19/9/42.
9012 (ex2430) 6/7/46.
9240 (ex3938) 27/1/50.
21052 (ex3478) 2/7/52.
21028 (ex3977) 11/11/54.
21018 (ex3943) 14/6/57.
28199 (ex3949) 7/3/59.
28394 (ex1127) 23/2/60.

SHEDS:
March.
Doncaster 25/6/50.
Frodingham 12/4/53.
Retford 3/1/54.

RENUMBERED:
3961 6/10/46.
63961 18/6/48.

CONDEMNED:
29/12/62.
Sold for scrap to Central Wagon
Co.Ince.

2437

Doncaster 1788.

To traffic 15/3/34.

REPAIRS:
Don. 22/8-30/9/35.**G.**
Don. 27/6-31/7/37.**G.**
Don. 7/1-4/2/39.**G.**
Don. 20/7-24/8/40.**G.**

Don. 4/4-16/5/42.**G.**
Don. 15/5-19/6/43.**L.**
Don. 6-27/5/44.**G.**
Don. 8-22/9/45.**L.**
Don. 11/5-8/6/46.**G.**
Don. 7/10-20/11/47.**G.**
Don. 3-19/12/47.**N/C.**
Don. 3-24/3/48.**L.**
Don. 19/12/49-19/1/50.**G.**
Don. 5/8-1/9/52.**G.**
Don. 29/12/52-22/1/53.**C/L.**
Don. 24/2-11/3/53.**N/C.**
Don. 27/3-28/4/55.**G.**
Don. 22/10-29/11/57.**G.**
Don. 23/1-17/2/62.**G.**

BOILERS:
4401.
4406 (ex2431) 4/2/39.
9437 (new) 27/5/44.
8820 (ex3939) 19/1/50.
21056 (ex3965) 1/9/52.
21066 (ex3966) 28/4/55.
21061 (ex3937) 29/11/57.
21047 (ex3936) 17/2/62.

SHEDS:
March.
New England 27/12/35.
March 4/1/36.
Doncaster 25/6/50.
Retford 16/9/62.
Grantham 30/12/62.
Doncaster 8/9/63.

RENUMBERED:
3962 27/10/46.
63962 24/3/48.

CONDEMNED:
22/9/63.
Sold for scrap to Bulwell Forest
Wagon Works.

3833

Doncaster 1931.

To traffic 22/5/42.

REPAIRS:
Don. 24/7-14/8/43.**L.**
Don. 8/7-5/8/44.**G.**
Don. 30/5-13/7/47.**G.**
Don. 20/2-13/4/50.**G.**
Don. 10/8-17/9/52.**G.**
Don. 23/11-22/12/54.**G.**
Don. 5/1-14/2/55.**C/L.**
Don. 19/1-20/2/58.**G.**
Don. 26/10-4/11/59.**N/C.**
Don. 25-26/1/61.**N/C.**
Don. 12/5-17/6/61.**G.**

BOILERS:
9314.
9363 (ex3960) 13/4/50.
21021 (ex3985) 17/9/52.
21000 (ex3959) 22/12/54.
21008 (ex3931) 20/2/58.
21010 (ex3985) 17/6/61.

SHEDS:
Doncaster.
Colwick 23/1/44.
New England 17/1/45.
Doncaster 11/12/45.
Frodingham 20/10/47.
Doncaster 13/6/54.
Grantham 14/6/59.

RENUMBERED:
3963 22/11/46.
63963 13/4/50.

CONDEMNED:
8/9/63.
Cut up at Doncaster.

3834

Doncaster 1932.

To traffic 10/6/42.

REPAIRS:
Don. 18-25/12/43.**L.**
Don. 22/7-12/8/44.**G.**
Don. 31/8-28/9/46.**G.**
Don. 6/4-12/5/48.**G.**
Don. 18/7-10/8/50.**G.**
Don. 10/2-10/3/53.**G.**
Don. 7/6-8/7/55.**C/H.**
Don. 16/7-18/8/56.**G.**
Don. 10/2-17/3/61.**G.**

BOILERS:
9315.
4401 (ex2954) 28/9/46.
9316 (ex3965) 10/8/50.
21064 (ex3959) 10/3/53.
21042 (ex3922) 18/8/56.
28331 (ex1165) 17/3/61.

SHEDS:
Doncaster.
Colwick 23/1/44.
Doncaster 9/12/45.
Langwith 27/10/46.
Doncaster 25/6/50.
Retford 31/1/60.

RENUMBERED:
3964 11/8/46.
63964 12/5/48.

CONDEMNED:
22/9/63.
Sold for scrap to Bulwell Forest
Wagon Works.

3835

Doncaster 1933.

To traffic 26/6/42.

REPAIRS:
Don. 19/9-10/10/42.**L.**
Don. 6-27/2/43.**L.**
Don. 3/6-15/7/44.**L.**
Don. 29/6-3/8/47.**G.**
Don. 9/10-9/11/49.**G.**
Don. 7/7-1/8/52.**G.**
Don. 6/10-5/11/54.**G.**
Don. 15/12/56-26/1/57.**G.**
Don. 6/8-5/9/59.**G.**
Don. 26/8-14/10/61.**L.**

BOILERS:
9316.
9364 (ex3949) 9/11/49.
21055 (ex3961) 1/8/52.
21058 (ex3972) 5/11/54.
21035 (ex3948) 26/1/57.
28963 (new) 5/9/59.

SHEDS:
Doncaster.
Colwick 23/1/44.
Langwith 5/10/47.
Grantham 18/6/50.
Mexborough 28/10/51.
Retford 17/2/52.

RENUMBERED:
3965 2/6/46.
63965 9/11/49.

CONDEMNED:
10/10/62.
Cut up at Doncaster.

3836

Doncaster 1934.

To traffic 31/7/42.

REPAIRS:
Don. 7-21/11/42.**L.**
Don. 11/11-2/12/44.**G.**
Don. 22/12/46-25/1/47.**G.**
Don. 9/10-5/11/47.**L.**
Don. 12/12/47-5/1/48.**G.**
Don. 8/3-8/4/49.**G.**
Don. 18/2-19/3/51.**G.**
Don. 20/4-13/5/53.**G.**

When the Thompson general re-numbering was able to be implemented from January 1946, O2 class became 3921 to 3987 in order of building date. Many had to be changed on Sundays, at their home sheds, using local labour, resulting in these 6" stencilled figures appearing. 3924 had been changed from 3479 at Doncaster shed on Sunday 16th June 1946, as seen here on the 22nd, but this method did not prove very durable. *A.G.Ellis.*

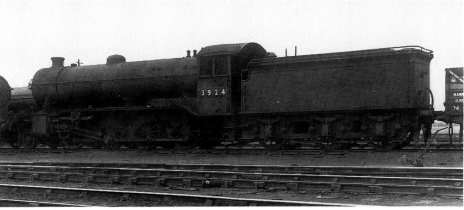

Don. 23/3-21/4/55.**G.**
Don. 19/12/57-24/1/58.**G.**
Don. 24/9-3/10/59.**N/C.**
Don. 16/8-24/9/60.**G.**

BOILERS:
9317.
8859 (*ex3923*) 8/4/49.
21017 (*ex3954*) 19/3/51.
21066 (*ex3964*) 13/5/53.
21032 (*ex3941*) 21/4/55.
28356 (*ex3950*) 24/1/58.
28445 (*ex1045*) 24/9/60.

SHEDS:
Doncaster.
Colwick 23/1/44.
Langwith 28/10/46.
Grantham 18/6/50.
Retford 11/6/61.

RENUMBERED:
3966 3/11/46.
63966 8/4/49.

CONDEMNED:
29/12/62.
Sold for scrap to Central Wagon Co.Ince.

3837

Doncaster 1935.

To traffic 21/8/42.

REPAIRS:
Don. 25/11-23/12/44.**G.**
Don. 12/11/46-11/1/47.**G.**
Don. 23/4-30/5/47.**L.**
Don. 28/9-5/11/48.**G.**
Don. 3-20/12/48.**L.**
Don. 16-29/12/49.**C/L.**
Don. 11/12/50-5/1/51.**G.**
Don. 14/8-18/9/53.**G.**

Don. 30/9-3/11/56.**G.**
Don. 14/5-5/6/58.**C/L.**
Don. 23/5-3/7/61.**G.**
Don. 9/11/62.*Not repaired.*

BOILERS:
9318.
9241 (*ex3929*) 5/11/48.
21012 (*ex3923*) 5/1/51.
21069 (*ex3935*) 18/9/53.
21046 (*ex3984*) 3/11/56.
21008 (*ex3963*) 3/7/61.

SHEDS:
Doncaster.
Colwick 23/1/44.
Langwith 20/10/46.
Doncaster 25/6/50.

RENUMBERED:
3967 15/9/46.
63967 5/11/48.

CONDEMNED:
26/11/62.
Cut up at Doncaster.

3838

Doncaster 1936.

To traffic 2/9/42.

REPAIRS:
Don. 26/12/42-16/1/43.**L.**
Don. 3-31/7/43.**L.**
Don. 23/12/44-3/2/45.**G.**
Don. 2-23/11/46.**G.**
Don. 9/6-16/7/48.**G.**
Don. 6-29/12/50.**G.**
Don. 13/10-10/11/52.**G.**
Don. 2-25/11/54.**C/L.**
Don. 22/8-29/9/55.**G.**
Don. 1/5-3/6/58.**G.**

Don. 19/11-1/12/60.**N/C.**
Don. 22/2-25/3/61.**G.**

BOILERS:
9319.
8976 (*ex3943*) 16/7/48.
21011 (*ex3986*) 29/12/50.
21062 (*ex3945*) 10/11/52.
21068 (*ex3949*) 29/9/55.
21070 (*ex3952*) 3/6/58.
28509 (*ex1254*) 25/3/61.

SHEDS:
Doncaster.
Colwick 23/1/44.
Langwith 5/10/47.
Doncaster 25/6/50.
Retford 9/12/62.
Grantham 30/12/62.
Doncaster 8/9/63.

RENUMBERED:
3968 1/9/46.
63968 16/7/48.

CONDEMNED:
22/9/63.
Cut up at Doncaster.

3839

Doncaster 1937.

To traffic 12/9/42.

REPAIRS:
Don. 23/12/44-3/2/45.**G.**
Don. 8-15/12/45.**L.**
Don. 12/11/46-11/1/47.**G.**
Don. 23/1-1/3/47.**L.**
Don. 20/2-25/3/49.**G.**
Don. 28/9-24/10/51.**G.**
Don. 14/8-25/9/53.**G.**
Don. 1-31/12/55.**G.**

Don. 4-8/10/57.**C/L.**
Don. 17/10-5/11/60.**N/C.**
Don. 31/8-23/11/61.**G.**
Don. 16/1-20/2/63.**C/L.**

BOILERS:
9320.
9323 (*ex3972*) 25/3/49.
21038 (*ex3975*) 24/10/51.
21006 (*ex3923*) 25/9/53.

SHEDS:
Doncaster.
Colwick 23/1/44.
Langwith 20/10/46.
Mexborough 2/7/50.
Doncaster 18/3/51.
Retford 31/1/60.

RENUMBERED:
3969 8/9/46.
63969 25/3/49.

CONDEMNED:
3/11/63.
Cut up at Doncaster.

3840

Doncaster 1938.

To traffic 21/9/42.

REPAIRS:
Don. 30/9-3/10/42.**L.**
Don. 17/3-21/4/45.**G.**
Don. 17/8-21/9/46.**G.**
Don. 6/1-6/2/48.**G.**
Don. 14/2-5/4/50.**G.**
Don. 24/9-17/10/52.**G.**
Don. 14/12/54-19/1/55.**G.**
Don. 11/11-20/12/57.**G.**
Don. 24-30/4/59.**C/L.**
Don. 22/4/60.*Not repaired.*

WORKS CODES:- Cow - Cowlairs. Dar - Darlington. Don - Doncaster. Ghd - Gateshead. Gor - Gorton. Inv - Inverurie. Str - Stratford.

REPAIR CODES:- **C/H** - Casual Heavy. **C/L** - Casual Light. **G** - General. **H** - Heavy. **H/I** - Heavy Intermediate. **L** - Light. **L/I** - Light Intermediate. **N/C** - Non-Classified.

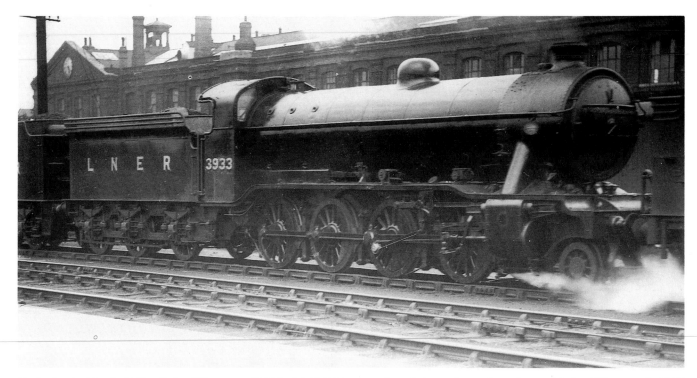

Beginning in March 1946, all the O2's except 3921 had L N E R restored to their tender, and on those with the GN type cab, 7¹/₂" instead of the normal 12" figures still had to be used. No. 3933 here ex works on 1st June 1946 is of particular interest because it has one of the ten class B tenders on which in 1923, an extra coal rail was fitted so as to give extra capacity to the 4-4-2 passenger engines to which they were then coupled.

BOILERS:
9321.
8974 (ex3948) 6/2/48.
9320 (ex3969) 5/4/50.
21060 (ex3982) 17/10/52.
21052 (ex3946) 20/12/57.

SHEDS:
Doncaster.
Colwick 23/1/44.
Langwith 20/10/46.
Annesley 20/2/48.
Langwith 7/3/48.
Mexborough 2/7/50.
Retford 5/8/51.

RENUMBERED:
3970 21/9/46.
E3970 6/2/48.
63970 5/4/50.

CONDEMNED:
9/5/60.
Cut up at Doncaster.

3841

Doncaster 1939.

To traffic 5/10/42.

REPAIRS:
Don. 10-24/4/43.**L.**
Don. 10/3-14/4/45.**G.**

Don. 10/12/46-18/1/47.**G.**
Don. 8/3-7/4/48.**L.**
Don. 5/12/48-7/1/49.**G.**
Don. 7/4-17/5/51.**G.**
Don. 5-29/5/53.**G.**
Don. 5-29/4/54.**C/L.**
Don. 27/4-25/5/55.**G.**
Don. 10/11-7/12/57.**G.**
Don. 23/7-26/8/60.**G.**

BOILERS:
9322.
8463 (ex3475) 7/1/49.
21023 (ex3983) 17/5/51.
21008 (ex3953) 29/5/53.
21011 (ex3976) 25/5/55.
21066 (ex3962) 7/12/57.
21035 (ex3965) 26/8/60.

SHEDS:
Doncaster.
Colwick 23/1/44.
Langwith 20/10/46.
Mexborough 2/7/50.
Doncaster 18/3/51.
Retford 27/4/58.

RENUMBERED:
3971 3/11/46.
63971 7/4/48.

CONDEMNED:
29/12/62.

Sold for scrap to Central Wagon Co.Ince.

3842

Doncaster 1940.

To traffic 10/10/42.
REPAIRS:
Don. 17/4-1/5/43.**L.**
Don. 22/4-27/5/44.**L.**
Don. 17/2-17/3/45.**G.**
Don. 3/11-21/12/46.**G.**
Don. 30/11-19/12/47.**L.**
Don. 14-24/12/48.**G.**
Don. 9/4-17/5/50.**G.**
Don. 20/8-23/9/52.**G.**
Don. 20/9-21/10/54.**G.**
Don. 28/1-9/3/57.**G.**
Don. 20/10-6/12/60.**G.**
Don. 20/3-5/4/62.**C/L.**

BOILERS:
9323.
9394 (ex3982) 24/12/48.
9398 (ex3986) 17/5/50.
21058 (ex3937) 23/9/52.
21040 (ex3938) 21/10/54.
21044 (ex3946) 6/12/60.

SHEDS:
Doncaster.
Colwick 23/1/44.

Langwith 20/10/46.
Mexborough 2/7/50.
Retford 5/8/51.

RENUMBERED:
3972 10/11/46.
63972 24/12/48.

CONDEMNED:
4/5/63.
Sold for scrap to Bulwell Forest Wagon Works.

3843

Doncaster 1941.

To traffic 23/10/42.

REPAIRS:
Don. 13-20/2/43.**L.**
Don. 7-21/10/44.**G.**
Don. 10/2-24/3/45.**L.**
Don. 23/3-11/5/47.**G.**
Don. 29/5-13/6/47.**L.**
Don. 31/10-30/11/48.**L.**
Don. 2/6-8/7/49.**G.**
Don. 27/9-30/10/51.**G.**
Don. 19/11-18/12/53.**G.**
Don. 8/1-11/2/56.**G.**
Don. 16/7-18/8/58.**G.**
Don. 27/7-8/8/59.**N/C.**
Don. 22/9-16/12/61.**G.**

After the 1st January 1948 change of ownership, tenders began to carry **BRITISH RAILWAYS**, and on the first four 3946/70/8/9, the number was given the E prefix. From March 24th when 63962 was ex works the figure 6 had replaced the E, and on double window cabs, 12" painted figures could be used, as seen on 63954 which was ex works 28th May 1948, just too soon to get smokebox cast number plate fitted. *E.V.Fry.*

BOILERS:
9385.
8975 *(ex3478)* 11/5/47.
9465 *(ex3925)* 8/7/49.
21039 *(ex3984)* 30/10/51.
21029 *(ex3951)* 18/12/53.
21007 *(ex3951)* 11/2/56.
21027 *(ex3974)* 18/8/58.
21009 *(ex3987)* 16/12/61.

SHEDS:
Doncaster.
Colwick 23/1/44.
Langwith 20/10/46.
Mexborough 2/7/50.
Doncaster 27/8/50.
Retford 16/10/60.

RENUMBERED:
3973 22/9/46.
63973 27/11/48.

CONDEMNED:
22/9/63.
Sold for scrap to Bulwell Forest Wagon Works.

3844

Doncaster 1942.

To traffic 3/11/42.

REPAIRS:
Don. 20/1-10/3/45.**G.**
Don. 13/7-17/8/46.**G.**
Don. 26/11-28/12/46.**H.**
Don. 7-31/12/47.**H.**
Don. 19/6-23/7/48.**L.**
Don. 25/5-22/6/49.**G.**
Don. 28/12/51-24/1/52.**G.**
Don. 10/4-12/5/54.**G.**
Don. 2/4-8/5/56.**G.**
Don. 20/6-30/7/58.**G.**
Don. 7-24/3/59.**C/L.**
Don. 3-18/10/60.**N/C.**
Don. 5/3-28/4/62.**G.**

BOILERS:
9386.
9470 *(new)* 28/12/46.
9013 *(ex3958)* 22/6/49.
21004 *(ex3956)* 24/1/52.
21030 *(ex3927)* 12/5/54.
21027 *(ex3987)* 8/5/56.
21043 *(ex3938)* 30/7/58.
21055 *(ex3959)* 28/4/62.

SHEDS:
Doncaster.
Colwick 23/1/44.
Langwith 20/10/46.
Mexborough 18/6/50.
Doncaster 27/8/50.
Grantham 28/10/62.
Doncaster 8/9/63.

RENUMBERED:
3974 16/8/46.
63974 23/7/48.

CONDEMNED:
22/9/63.
Sold for scrap to Bulwell Forest Wagon Works.

3845

Doncaster 1943.

To traffic 6/11/42.

REPAIRS:
Don. 16/9-7/10/44.**G.**
Don. 19/10-2/11/46.**G.**
Don. 13/1-11/2/49.**G.**

Don. 7/9-10/10/51.**G.**
Don. 25/3-23/4/53.**C/L.**
Don. 12/1-6/2/54.**G.**
Don. 28/5-7/6/55.**C/L.**
Don. 5/3-6/4/56.**G.**
Don. 11/6-12/7/57.**C/L.**
Don. 16/8-27/9/58.**G.**
Don. 3-23/1/59.**C/L.**
Don. 27/8-5/9/59.**N/C.**
Don. 18/5-12/7/62.**G.**

BOILERS:
9387.
9161 *(ex3458)* 2/11/46.
9319 *(ex3968)* 11/2/49.
21036 *(ex3987)* 10/10/51.
21039 *(ex3973)* 6/2/54.
21009 *(ex3934)* 6/4/56.
21020 *(ex3958)* 27/9/58.
28525 *(ex1009)* 12/7/62.

SHEDS:
Doncaster.
New England 21/11/42.
Doncaster 11/12/45.
Frodingham 20/10/47.
Langwith 12/3/50.
Mexborough 2/7/50.
Doncaster 18/3/51.
Retford 16/10/60.

RENUMBERED:
3975 2/11/46.
63975 11/2/49.

CONDEMNED:
3/11/63.
Cut up at Doncaster.

3846

Doncaster 1944.

To traffic 18/11/42.

REPAIRS:
Don. 5/2-25/3/44.**L.**
Don. 19/8-16/9/44.**G.**
Don. 25/11-23/12/44.**L.**
Don. 17/8-21/9/46.**G.**
Don. 11/6-16/7/47.**H.**

Don. 14/4-20/5/48.**G.**
Don. 2/6-12/7/50.**G.**
Don. 4-12/6/51.**C/L.**
Don. 4/12/52-2/1/53.**G.**
Don. 1/6-2/7/54.**C/L.**
Don. 19/4-20/5/55.**G.**
Don. 4/2-1/3/58.**G.**
Don. 15/11-16/12/60.**G.**

BOILERS:
9388.
9315 (ex3964) 16/7/47.

9164 (ex3948) 12/7/50.
21011 (ex3968) 2/1/53.
21056 (ex3962) 20/5/55.
21054 (ex3923) 1/3/58.
28364 (ex1152) 16/12/60.

SHEDS:
Doncaster.
New England 21/11/42.
Doncaster 28/12/45.
Langwith 27/10/46.
Mexborough 16/7/50.

As from September 1946, no.3487 was re-numbered 3932, and in October 1944 it had been one of the five which were changed to Diagram 100A boiler. That did not have any effect on its light alloy connecting rods, and after it was ex works in December 1951, there was no further report on the rods, except one in January 1952 recording that only the outside rods were Hiduminium, the inside one being conventional steel. *British Railways.*

Retford 5/8/57.

RENUMBERED:
3976 21/9/46.
63976 20/5/48.

CONDEMNED:
22/9/63.
Cut up at Doncaster.

3847

Doncaster 1945.

To traffic 21/11/42.

REPAIRS:
Don. 31/3-5/5/45.**G.**
Don. 9/6-7/7/45.**L.**
Don. 13/12/46-25/1/47.**G.**
Don. 23/1-18/2/49.**G.**
Don. 7/6-9/7/51.**G.**

Don. 27/9-22/10/54.**G.**
Don. 22/5-11/6/58.**C/L.**
Don. 11-23/8/58.**C/L.**
Don. 26/9-18/11/60.**G.**

BOILERS:
9389.
9386 *(ex3974)* 25/1/47.
9161 *(ex3975)* 18/2/49.
21028 *(ex3971)* 9/7/51.
21049 *(ex3948)* 22/10/54.
21053 *(ex3937)* 18/11/60.

SHED:
Doncaster.

RENUMBERED:
3977 24/11/46.
63977 18/2/49.

CONDEMNED:
22/9/63.
Sold for scrap to Bulwell Forest Wagon Works.

3848

Doncaster 1946.

To traffic 28/11/42.

REPAIRS:
Don. 24/2-24/3/45.**G.**
Don. 5/1-19/2/47.**G.**
Don. 5/11-10/12/47.**H.**
Don. 20/1-6/2/48.**L.**
Don. 6/4-6/5/49.**G.**
Don. 11/8-5/9/51.**G.**
Don. 26/7-28/8/53.**G.**
Don. 8/6-16/7/55.**G.**
Don. 17-29/5/57.**C/L.**
Don. 14/2-21/3/58.**G.**
Don. 18-28/8/59.**N/C.**
Don. 13/1-16/2/61.**G.**
Don. 5-13/3/63.**C/L.**

BOILERS:
9390.
8183 (ex2431) 19/2/47.
21033 (ex3483) 5/9/51.
21015 (ex3958) 28/8/53.
21014 (ex3928) 16/7/55.
21056 (ex3976) 21/3/58.
21067 (ex3941) 16/2/61.

SHEDS:
Doncaster.
Colwick 23/1/44.
Langwith 20/10/46.
Mexborough 2/7/50.
Doncaster 18/3/51.
Retford 16/9/62.

RENUMBERED:
3978 14/12/46.
63978 6/5/49.

CONDEMNED:
7/5/63.
Cut up at Doncaster.

3849

Doncaster 1947.

To traffic 4/12/42.

REPAIRS:
Don. 17/3-21/4/45.**G.**
Don. 9-30/11/46.**G.**
Don. 28/12/47-23/1/48.**H.**
Don. 13/12/48-17/1/49.**G.**
Don. 13/10-12/11/51.**G.**
Don. 11/2-10/3/54.**G.**

Don. 26/7-30/8/56.**G.**
Don. 15/5-13/6/59.**G.**
Don. 20/12/60-6/1/61.**N/C.**
Don. 3/9/62.Not repaired.
BOILERS:
9391.
9160 (ex2433) 30/11/46.
9243 (ex3926) 17/1/49.
21041 (ex3969) 12/11/51.
21001 (ex3943) 10/3/54.
21064 (ex3964) 30/8/56.
28111 (ex3924) 13/6/59.

SHEDS:
Doncaster.
Colwick 25/1/44.
Langwith 5/10/47.
Mexborough 2/7/50.
Doncaster 18/3/51.
Retford 17/8/52.

RENUMBERED:
3979 22/11/46.
E3979 23/1/48.
63979 17/1/49.

CONDEMNED:
10/9/62.
Cut up at Doncaster.

3850

Doncaster 1948.

To traffic 11/12/42.

REPAIRS:
Don. 24/2-31/3/45.**G.**
Don. 12/1-15/2/47.**G.**
Don. 18/11-24/12/47.**L.**
Don. 7/3-16/4/48.**G.**
Don. 5-31/5/49.**G.**
Don. 5-28/11/51.**G.**
Don. 1-26/3/54.**G.**
Don. 23/5-5/7/56.**G.**
Don. 17/2-20/3/59.**G.**
Don. 26/10-13/11/59.**C/L.**
Don. 30-31/1/61.**N/C.**
Don. 10/8-22/11/61.**G.**

BOILERS:
9392.
4407 (ex spare) 31/5/49.
21042 (ex3979) 28/11/51.
21036 (ex3975) 26/3/54.
21005 (ex3930) 5/7/56.

SHEDS:
Doncaster.

Colwick 23/1/44.
Langwith 20/10/46.
Mexborough 2/7/50.
Doncaster 25/2/51.
Retford 17/8/52.

RENUMBERED:
3980 8/12/46.
63980 16/4/48.

CONDEMNED:
22/9/63.
Sold for scrap to Bulwell Forest
Wagon Works.

3851

Doncaster 1949.

To traffic 17/12/42.

REPAIRS:
Don. 8/5-19/6/43.**L.**
Don. 4-18/3/44.**L.**
Don. 21/10-4/11/44.**G.**
Don. 18/11-2/12/44.**L.**
Don. 6/2-24/3/47.**G.**
Don. 19/4-12/5/48.**L.**
Don. 29/12/48-14/1/49.**G.**
Don. 2-31/5/51.**G.**
Don. 3/3-2/4/54.**G.**
Don. 29/9-30/10/57.**G.**
Don. 1-10/3/61.**N/C.**
Don. 19/10-9/12/61.**G.**

BOILERS:
9393.
9391 (ex spare and 3979) 14/1/
49.
21025 (ex3934) 31/5/51.
21034 (ex3987) 2/4/54.
21057 (ex3959) 30/10/57.
21031 (ex3927) 9/12/61.

SHEDS:
Doncaster.
Colwick 23/1/44.
Langwith 20/10/46.
Mexborough 2/7/50.
Doncaster 14/9/52.
Grantham 28/10/62.
Retford 8/9/63.

RENUMBERED:
3981 20/10/46.
63981 12/5/48.

CONDEMNED:
3/11/63.
Cut up at Doncaster.

3852

Doncaster 1950.

To traffic 21/12/42.

REPAIRS:
Don. 27/3-10/4/43.**L.**
Don. 4/11-2/12/44.**G.**
Don. 30/12/44-20/1/45.**L.**
Don. 26/10-22/11/46.**G.**
Don. 25/5-24/6/48.**G.**
Don. 16/4-15/5/50.**G.**
Don. 30/4-10/5/51.**C/L.**
Don. 8/8-16/9/52.**G.**
Don. 3/1-12/2/53.**C/L.**
Don. 15/10-10/11/54.**G.**
Don. 1-4/8/56.**N/C.**
Don. 1/7-9/8/57.**G.**
Don. 23/1-27/2/60.**G.**
Don. 1-3/2/61.**N/C.**

BOILERS:
9394.
9390 (ex3478) 24/6/48.
8855 (ex3945) 15/5/50.
21057 (ex3482) 16/9/52.
21055 (ex3965) 10/11/54.
28352 (ex1175) 9/8/57.
28570 (ex1645) 27/2/60.

SHEDS:
Doncaster.
Colwick 23/1/44.
Langwith 5/10/47.
Mexborough 2/7/50.
Retford 5/8/51.
Grantham 20/11/60.

RENUMBERED:
3982 17/10/46.
63982 24/6/48.

CONDEMNED:
9/12/62.
Sold for scrap to
F.C.Larkinson,Grantham.

3853

Doncaster 1951.

To traffic 26/12/42.

WORKS CODES:- Cow - Cowlairs. Dar - Darlington. Don - Doncaster. Ghd - Gateshead. Gor - Gorton. Inv - Inverurie. Str - Stratford.

REPAIR CODES:- **C/H** - Casual Heavy. **C/L** - Casual Light. **G** - General. **H** - Heavy. **H/I** - Heavy Intermediate. **L** - Light. **L/I** - Light Intermediate. **N/C** - Non-Classified.

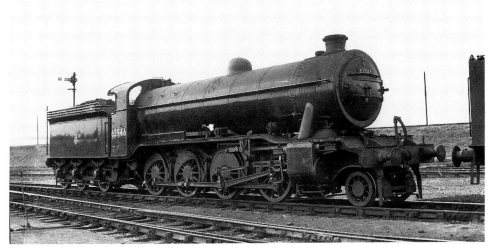

Using the 10" un-shaded figures, that size could just be accommodated on the short side of those which still had the original GN cab. Note that 63946 is another O2 coupled with one of the class B tenders to which an extra coal rail was added in 1923. After being coupled with this O2 from March 1943 until August 1960, it was then converted into a mobile snowplough, for use with diesel locomotives. *A.G.Ellis.*

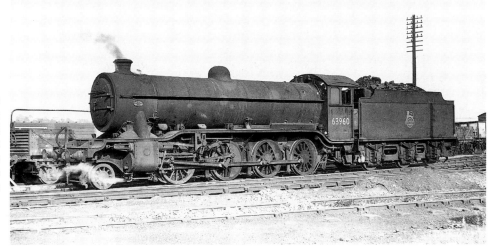

There were two standard sizes of lion over a wheel emblem used from September 1949. On those coupled with the Group Standard 4200 gallon type tender, the 28" emblem was used, irrespective of whether the tender was flush sided, or had a stepped top. *P.H.Groom.*

REPAIRS:
Don. 5/5-9/6/45.**G.**
Don. 13/4-4/5/46.**L.**
Don. 19/10-21/12/46.**G.**
Don. 24/3-4/5/47.**G.**
Don. 15/10-25/11/48.**G.**
Don. 5/3-4/4/51.**G.**
Don. 22/10-14/11/53.**G.**
Don. 8/6-21/7/56.**G.**
Don. 14/7-20/8/60.**G.**

BOILERS:
9395.
  9245 *(ex3946)* 25/11/48.
21018 *(ex3966)* 4/4/51.
21024 *(ex3952)* 14/11/53.
28190 *(ex1641)* 21/7/56.
28574 *(ex1033)* 20/8/60.

SHEDS:
Doncaster.
Colwick 23/1/44.
Langwith 20/10/46.
Mexborough 2/7/50.
Frodingham 17/8/52.
Doncaster 13/6/54.
Retford 16/10/60.

RENUMBERED:
  3983 4/5/46.
63983 25/11/48.

CONDEMNED:
2/7/63.
Cut up at Doncaster.

3854

Doncaster 1952.

To traffic 31/12/42.

REPAIRS:
Don. 27/1-10/3/45.**G.**
Don. 6/4-19/5/47.**G.**
Don. 10/8-17/9/48.**G.**
Don. 7/5-1/6/51.**G.**
Don. 21-24/8/51.**N/C.**
Don. 30/6-23/7/54.**G.**
Don. 20/9-31/10/56.**G.**
Don. 10/6-27/7/60.**C/H.**
Don. 31/1-3/3/62.**G.**

BOILERS:
9396.
  9016 *(ex3468)* 19/5/47.
21026 *(ex3978)* 1/6/51.
21046 *(ex3936)* 23/7/54.
21036 *(ex3980)* 31/10/56.

SHEDS:
Doncaster.
Colwick 23/1/44.
New England 29/3/44.
Doncaster 18/11/45.
Langwith 27/10/46.
Mexborough 2/7/50.
Frodingham 17/8/52.
Doncaster 29/8/54.
Retford 16/9/62.
Grantham 30/12/62.
Retford 8/9/63.

RENUMBERED:
  3984 1/12/46.
63984 17/9/48.

CONDEMNED:
3/11/63.
Cut up at Doncaster.

3855

Doncaster 1953.

To traffic 2/1/43.

REPAIRS:
Don. 5/5-2/6/45.**G.**
Don. 10/2-28/3/47.**G.**
Don. 5-21/5/48.**L.**
Don. 6/1-9/2/49.**G.**
Don. 3-26/4/51.**G.**
Don. 11-25/5/51.**C/L.**
Don. 10/1-11/2/52.**C/H.**
Don. 26/4-21/5/54.**G.**
Don. 24/9-1/11/56.**C/L.**
Don. 14/5-13/6/58.**G.**
Don. 29/9-8/10/60.**N/C.**
Don. 3/4-6/5/61.**G.**

BOILERS:
9397.
  9160 *(ex3979)* 9/2/49.
21021 *(ex3926)* 26/4/51.
21047 *(ex3951)* 11/2/52.
21031 *(ex3922)* 21/5/54.
21010 *(ex3933)* 13/6/58.

Those engines which had the 3500 gallon GN class B tender got the smaller 15¹/₂" tall type. *British Railways.*

21059 *(ex3942)* 6/5/61.

SHEDS:
Doncaster.
Colwick 23/1/44.
Doncaster 9/12/45.
Langwith 27/10/46.
Mexborough 2/7/50.
Frodingham 17/8/52.
Doncaster 13/6/54.
Retford 16/9/62.
Grantham 30/12/62.
Retford 8/9/63.

RENUMBERED:
 3985 4/10/46.
63985 21/5/48.

CONDEMNED:
22/9/63.
Sold for scrap to Bulwell Forest
Wagon Works.

3856

Doncaster 1954.

To traffic 7/1/43.

REPAIRS:
Don. 6/1-24/2/45.**G.**
Don. 23/3-6/5/47.**G.**
Don. 29/5-5/7/49.**G.**
Don. 23/10-29/11/50.**G.**
Don. 20/9-24/10/53.**G.**
Don. 1/3-13/4/55.**C/L.**
Don. 8/12/55-10/1/56.**G.**
Don. 28/10-5/12/58.**G.**
Don. 30/1-28/2/61.**G.**
Don. 12-19/9/61.**C/L.**

BOILERS:
 9398.
 9393 *(ex3981)* 5/7/49.
21009 *(ex3946)* 29/11/50.
21038 *(ex3969)* 24/10/53.
21063 *(ex3927)* 5/12/58.
21052 *(ex3970)* 28/2/61.

SHEDS:
Doncaster.
Colwick 23/1/44.
New England 29/3/44.
Doncaster 18/12/45.
Langwith 27/10/46.
Mexborough 2/7/50.
Doncaster 27/8/50.
Retford 17/8/52.

RENUMBERED:
 3986 17/11/46.
63986 5/7/49.

CONDEMNED:
7/6/63.*Cut up at Doncaster.*

3857

Doncaster 1955.

To traffic 21/1/43.

REPAIRS:
Don. 9/6-21/7/45.**G.**
Don. 30/3-20/4/46.**L.**
Don. 31/8-7/9/46.**L.**
Don. 27/7-28/8/47.**G.**
Don. 18/5-16/6/49.**G.**
Don. 26/8-26/9/51.**G.**
Don. 20/1-15/2/54.**G.**
Don. 5/3-24/4/56.**G.**
Don. 26/11-30/12/58.**G.**
Don. 25/6-16/7/59.**C/L.**
Don. 5-9/10/59.**N/C.**
Don. 30/10-14/12/61.**G.**

BOILERS:
 9399.
 9386 *(ex3977)* 16/6/49.
21034 *(ex3941)* 26/9/51.
21027 *(ex3925)* 15/2/54.
21039 *(ex3975)* 24/4/56.
21009 *(ex3975)* 30/12/58.
21057 *(ex3981)* 14/12/61.

SHEDS:
Doncaster.
Colwick 23/1/44.
New England 29/3/44.
Doncaster 18/12/45.
Langwith 27/10/46.
Annesley 20/2/48.
Langwith 7/3/48.
Mexborough 7/2/50.
Doncaster 27/8/50.
Retford 17/8/52.
Grantham 30/12/62.
Retford 8/9/63.

RENUMBERED:
 3987 19/4/46.
63987 16/6/49.

CONDEMNED:
22/9/63. *Sold for scrap to
Bulwell Forest Wagon Works.*

No.484 built by N.B.Loco.Co. in July 1921 was the engine chosen for special painting to be shown to the Directors on the Locomotive Committee at York on 31st January 1923 when they were deliberating on standard liveries for LNER locomotives. It was repainted from grey with white lining to black with red lining, but retained GN style transfer figures on its cab. That was duplicated on the tender in 12" shaded figures below the new Company's initials, but including the ampersand, and 484 was the only O2 to have that applied. It then kept ampersand until it went into works for general repair on 29th August 1923.

Here is an exceedingly rare (possibly unique) occurrence of all three tender types coupled with O2 class being seen, in traffic, together. No. 63983 had double window cab and flush sided tender, 63945 had both GN cab and tender, whilst 63966 had side window cab but a tender with stepped top. They were seen at Crowden, returning to their home shed of Langwith, and the preparations for the Manchester to Sheffield electrification will be noted. *P.J.Lynch.*

The prototype of the class, seen here in 1934 at Hadley Wood on a coal train for London, was still engaged on the work for which it had been designed 15 years previously. 3461 carried this double dome boiler from February 1929 until October 1935, but the feed water into it only from November 1933. In addition to having different cylinder and valve gear arrangement, it was the only one of the 67 in the class to be fitted with footsteps at the front end.

At the end of the 1939-45 war many of the class were switched from the London coal traffic to taking iron ore from Northamptonshire to both the furnaces in North Lincolnshire, and as far as York to those on Tees-side, for which they were transferred to work from Grantham shed. Unrecognisable here in August 1961 as the number 484 shown to the Directors at York in January 1923, that engine is leaving the main line at High Dyke to take empty iron ore wagons on to the Stainby goods branch, for which single line working it had tablet exchange apparatus. *L.Perrin.*

3499 here in March 1933 is taking another train of coal from Peterborough to London and making it very evident that hard work was involved. It was fitted with this Gresham feed water heater from August 1931 until September 1937.

3500 worked from New England shed for 21½ years from new in May 1924, entirely to and from London, and here on Werrington troughs is on a train of coal empties, being returned to pits in Nottinghamshire. It was the only O2 fitted with Dabeg feed water heater, that equipment being clearly seen on its left hand side.

CLASS P1

2393

Doncaster 1619.

To traffic 27/6/25.

REPAIRS:
Don. 15-22/8/25.**L.**
Don. 22/2-23/3/27.**L.**
Don. 25/6-1/9/28.**G.** *Dry sand to leading wheels.*
Don. 2-24/7/29.**L.**
Don. 5/8-24/10/31.**G.**
Don. 7/3-4/4/32.**L.** *Repairs to booster.*
Don. 22/3-12/5/34.**G.**
Don. 22/7-29/8/35.**L.**
Don. 22/10/35-3/3/36.**L.**
Don. 8/1-20/2/37.**G.** *Booster cyls from 4419.*
Don. 27/5-4/6/37.**L.** *Booster dismantled.*
Don. 13-31/5/38.**L.** *Booster removed.*
Don. 13/4-18/5/40.**G.**
Don. 9-23/5/42.**L.**
Don. 12/12/42-23/1/43.**G.** *220lb.boiler.*
Don. 10-24/7/43.**L.**

BOILERS:
7779.
7699 *(ex4475 and spare)* 12/5/34.
8251 *(ex2573)* 23/1/43.

SHEDS:
Doncaster.
New England 29/7/25.

CONDEMNED:
24/7/45.
Cut up at Doncaster.

2394

MLS superheater E type.
Doncaster 1620.

To traffic 14/11/25.

REPAIRS:
Don. 19-21/11/25.**L.**
Don. 5-16/8/27.**L.**
Don. 11/10-24/11/27.**L.** *Dry sand to leading.wheels.*
Don. 21/2-18/6/28.**H.**
Don. 14/9-17/11/31.**G.** *Robinson 32 element superheater fitted instead.*
Don. 19/4-3/5/32.**L.**
Don. 4/6-27/7/34.**G.**
Don. 17/7-26/8/36.**L.**
Don. 23/2-8/4/37.**G.** *Booster removed.*
Don. 2/3-13/4/40.**G.**
Don. 11-25/10/41.**L.**
Don. 26/9-31/10/42.**G.** *220lb.boiler.*
Don. 30/6/45. *Not repaired.*

BOILERS:
7782.
7802 *(ex2568)* 27/7/34.
7695 *(ex2561)* 8/4/37.
8783 *(ex2507 and spare)* 31/10/42.

SHEDS:
Doncaster.
New England 2/12/25.

CONDEMNED:
5/7/45.
Cut up at Doncaster.

The second engine was not put into traffic until November 1925, and differed only in the type of superheater which was fitted. Instead of the usual Robinson type with 32 elements, a trial of an "E Double" was made on it, and that required twin Gresley anti-vacuum to be fitted behind the chimney, also a larger access cover. *L.N.E.R.*

Both engines were fitted with a booster engine to drive their trailing carrying wheels, ostensibly to help them get 100-wagon trains on the move from a halt in refuge sidings, and this shows its arrangement. There were three articulated couplings in the steam supply pipe to permit vertical movement, and side play, but the cast iron pipes near to the ball & socket joints needed frequent replacement from breakages, aggravated by the very tight curves of the triangle used for turning the engines at New England shed where both were allocated. *L.N.E.R.*

The special superheater on 2394 was found to give only a marginal temperature rise to the superheated steam, so when 2394 was in works for a general repair late in 1931, that superheater was taken out and replaced, in the same boiler, by a standard 32 element Robinson superheater, and normal single anti-vacuum valve, and access cover were fitted.

Although 2393 had a change of boiler during its May 1934 repair, the replacement being from a Pacific, it was still one which worked at 180 lb pressure, and had a round dome cover. At the end of 1942, no.2393 had another change of boiler, and by then only the 220 lb type were available, but again 2393 got one with a round dome cover, which it then kept to its July 1945 withdrawal. *A.F.Cook.*

2394's boiler was changed in July 1934, and again in April 1937, and both replacements, which came from Pacifics, worked at 180 lb and had a round dome cover. A further change made in October 1942, put the working pressure to 220 lb and was one which had the 'banjo' type steam collector, which 2394 then retained to its withdrawal. *A.F.Cook.*

(left) All the booster equipment was removed from 2394 when it went for repair in February 1937, but in that month, 2393 left works fitted with the booster cylinders taken from Atlantic no.4419. However in May 1938 no.2393 also had booster removed, and although subsequent photographs are scarce, this one shows it at Hadley Wood on 24th July 1941. *A.R.Goult.*

(middle) Originally the cab sides were of the same design as on the Pacifics, with the depth of cut out matching that of the windows, and not until during 1934 were sight screens fitted. When seat backs in the cab were added in 1937, the cut out was reduced by 11", and an 8" longer vertical handrail was fitted. Both engines had, and kept, right-hand driving position, and were steam braked, with vacuum ejector for train braking. The Westinghouse pump had no connection with braking - it was only for operating the booster, and was removed along with that equipment. This photograph at Welwyn on 19th March 1938 must be one of the last to show a P1 fitted with booster, because by then 2394 had been deprived, and 2393 went to works on 13th May when it too had all its booster installation taken off. *H.C.Casserley.*

(bottom) Just ahead of the cab there was a difference of detail between the two engines. On 2394 the steam reverser operating rod was cranked above the trailing coupled wheels, but on 2393 it was straight. On both, sanding was only fitted for forward running, applicable in front of the two leading pairs of coupled wheels, and also to the booster wheels, at first all operated by steam. In November 1927, the leading sanders on 2394 were changed to gravity type, 2393 being altered similarly when out on 1st September 1928. That change led to the rod operating the leading sanders being visible across the lower part of the firebox. This 1937 picture shows 2394 soon after removal of its booster. By then both were in unlined black, the single red lining becoming a casualty of the June 1928 economies. This pair were allocated 3990 and 3991 when Thompson drew up his renumbering scheme in December 1943, but neither survived to take those numbers. *W.Potter.*

Here in 1927 at Hadley Wood, 2393 was doing the job for which it had been designed, the haulage of trains of up to 100 loaded wagons from Peterborough to Ferme Park yard in north London. Whilst the engine proved fully capable of doing that work, the refuge sidings on that line were totally inadequate in length for loads of that size to be put into them to allow faster trains to overtake. So it is no surprise that the class was never extended beyond the initial pair.

Still on the same work seven years later, 2393 now shows some detail differences. Cab sight screens have been added, the works plate on smokebox side, and the running number plate on the cab side have both disappeared, the open access hole in the front apron plate now has a hinged cover fitted, a cast collar showing load class 9 has been put on to the vacuum standpipe, the smokebox door hinge straps have been extended to prevent the door swinging too far open, the operating rod for the change to gravity sanding can be seen across the lower part of the firebox, and with change of number position from tender to cab side there was simultaneous loss of any lining on the black paint. So those two photographs do *NOT* duplicate each other.

2394 in January 1933 on the up slow line, and passing the water troughs at Langley, shows some - but not all - of the differences mentioned for 2393. It still carries the brass Doncaster works number plate on its smokebox side, and had yet to be fitted with sight screens on cab side, and the cover plate to prevent ash being able to get at the 2 to 1 levers. The chimney exhaust shows clear evidence of the effort which had to be exerted to move these heavy loads of coal.

Although not sharply focused, and probably taken hurriedly and riskily, because the date is 4th May 1940, this would be one of the last P1 action photographs. The return empty wagon trains were also rated as up to 100 being taken but their double lamp indication showed they ran as class B trains. The loaded up trains ran Mondays to Saturdays and left New England at 9.25 a.m., then on Tuesdays to Saturdays the empties left Ferme Park at 5.30 a.m., but on Sundays only at 5.00 a.m. so this picture must have been taken about 6 o'clock on a Saturday morning. *R.C.Riley.*

Almost six years later than when seen in the photograph opposite, actually on 22nd October 1938, and with a similar load, 2394 is able to coast down the 1 in 200, having reached the London side of the Potters Bar summit. By then, its special superheater, and its booster fittings were just memories, and its daily chore had settled into simply routine. These loaded up coal trains all ran with the single lamp indication that they were class C.

With 2393 having been treated to appearance in the Darlington celebration of 1925, evidently someone decided that its partner should at least have a modest share of the limelight. Although it was more than a year since it had received attention at Doncaster works, Peterborough spruced 2394 sufficiently for participation in a rolling stock exhibition at Cambridge on 7th and 8th May 1938 where it was seen by an attendance of 20,405. Oh happy days.

2001's opposite side, to the view on page 5, is shown because the engine was unusual in being equipped with a very neat, and tidy arrangement of A.C.F.I. feed water heater. It proved to be the only one of the class of six to be so fitted.

2001 also had single smoke and steam deflector plates fitted as an integral part of its boiler casing, and they were similar to those which had been introduced in 1929 on the high-pressure water tube boiler of the experimental no.10000. Here the engine is being turned by hand on the King's Cross station turntable.

CLASS P2

2001

Doncaster 1789.

To traffic 22/5/34.

REPAIRS:
Don. 24-27/8/34.**L.** *Tablet app.fitted.*
Don. 10-17/9/34.**L.** *New L.H.Piston.*
Don. 1-24/11/34.**L.** *Prepared for visit to Vitry.*
Don. 23/2-30/3/35.**L.** *New oil cooling arrgt fitted to R.C.gears.*
Don. 24-31/5/35.**L.**
Cow. 20/12/35.**H.**
Don. 27/5-7/7/36.**G.**
Don. 15/4-14/5/37.**G.**
Don. 30/9-14/4/38.**G.** *Rebuilt & streamlined.*
Don. 21/5-3/6/38.**L.** *New middle con.rod.*
Don. 13-15/9/38.**L.** *Boiler repairs.*
Cow. 25/3/39.**L.**
Don. 1/7-19/8/39.**G.**
Don. 30/12/39-13/1/40.**L.**
Don. 13/7-17/8/40.**G.**
Cow. 13-20/12/40.**L.**
Cow. 4-5/4/41.**L.**
Don. 7/3-25/4/42.**G.**
Cow. 16/10/43.**H.**
Cow. 25/4/44.**L.**
Don. 24/6/44. *for rebuilding.*

BOILER:
8771.

SHEDS:
Doncaster.
Haymarket 31/7/34.
Vitry (France) 5/12/34.
Haymarket 21/2/35.

Withdrawn and Rebuilt to Class A2/2.

2002

Doncaster 1796.

To traffic 6/10/34.

REPAIRS:
Don. 3-19/1/35.**L.** *New pyrometer.*

Don. 15/3-17/4/35.**L.** *Additional smoke deflectors.*
Don. 23/5-4/6/35.**L.**
Cow. 8/1-12/3/36.**L.**
Cow. 2-30/6/36.**L.**
Don. 7/8-14/10/36.**G.** *Streamlined front.*
Cow. 21-25/12/36.**L.**
Don. 13/8-4/9/37.**G.**
Cow. 28/10-5/11/37.**L.**
Cow. 21/6-22/7/38.**L.**
Don. 29/10-10/12/38.**G.**
Don. 24/2-20/4/40.**G.**
Don. 14/9-19/10/40.**G.**
Don. 15/11-6/12/41.**L.**
Don. 28/3-2/5/42.**H.**
Cow. 3-24/11/42.**L.**
Cow. 9-12/1/43.**L.**
Cow. 12-25/7/43.**L.**
Cow. 25/8-7/10/43.**L.**
Cow. 1-19/2/44.**L.**
Don. 1/4/44. *for rebuilding.*

BOILERS:
8785.
8797 *(new from spare)* 20/4/40.

SHEDS:
Doncaster.
Haymarket 9/6/35.
Dundee 22/6/35.
Aberdeen 10/9/36.

Withdrawn and Rebuilt to Class A2/2.

2003

Doncaster 1836.

To traffic 13/6/36.

REPAIRS:
Cow. 6-15/10/36.**L.**
Cow. 27/5-4/6/37.**L.**
Cow. 29/7-9/8/37.**L.**
Don. 11/3-9/4/38.**G.**
Cow. 25-28/5/38.**N/C.**
Cow. 8-15/6/38.**L.**
Don. 13-27/9/38.**L.**
Don. 3/6-15/7/39.**L.**
Don. 9/9-4/11/39.**G.**
Cow. 25-30/5/40.**L.**
Don. 18/1-8/3/41.**G.**
Cow. 18-21/8/41.**L.**
Cow. 23/9-4/10/41.**L.**
Don. 7/2-21/3/42.**L.**
Cow. 10/10-12/12/42.**G.**

Cow. 4-8/3/43.**L.**
Don. 2/9/44. *for rebuilding.*

BOILERS:
8796.
8785 *(ex2002)* 12/12/42.

SHEDS:
Haymarket.
Dundee 4/9/36.
Haymarket 23/10/42.
N.E.Area 27/11/42.
Haymarket 20/3/44.

Withdrawn and Rebuilt to Class A2/2.

2004

Doncaster 1839.

To traffic 11/7/36.

REPAIRS:
Cow. 24/2-3/3/37.**L.**
Don. 26/6-30/7/37.**L.**
Don. 27/1-7/3/38.**G.**
Cow. 3-10/8/38.**L.**
Cow. 10-16/1/39.**L.**
Don. 22/4-15/6/39.**L.**
Don. 6/12/39-2/2/40.**G.**
Don. 7/11-17/12/40.**L.**
Don. 23/4-7/6/41.**G.**
Cow. 28/12/42-26/2/43.**H.**
Don. 22/8/44. *for rebuilding.*

BOILER:
8798.

SHED:
Haymarket.

Withdrawn and Rebuilt to Class A2/2.

2005.

Doncaster 1840.

To traffic 8/8/36.

REPAIRS:
Cow. 11-21/12/36.**L.**
Don. 5/7-5/8/37.**L.**
Don. 8/11-22/12/37.**G.**
Cow. 7-12/1/38.**L.**
Don. 5/9-21/10/38.**G.**

Cow. 27-29/4/39.**L.**
Cow. 3-5/7/39.**L.**
Don. 8-26/8/39.**H.**
Cow. 2-7/2/40.**L.**
Cow. 24/4-2/5/40.**L.**
Don. 25/6-29/7/40.**G.**
Cow. 17-24/10/40.**L.**
Cow. 27/9-7/10/41.**L.**
Cow. 23-28/3/42.**L.**
Cow. 12-29/5/42.**L/I.**
Don. 26/10/42. *for rebuilding.*

BOILER:
8799.

SHED:
Dundee.

Withdrawn and Rebuilt to Class A2/2.

2006

Doncaster 1842.

To traffic 5/9/36.

REPAIRS:
Cow. 27/7-3/8/37.**L.**
Don. 7/10-19/11/37.**L.**
Don. 8/3-1/4/38.**L.**
Don. 2/5-3/7/39.**G.**
Don. 15/4-14/5/40.**H.**
Don. 29/10-14/12/40.**H.**
Don. 23/9-13/11/41.**G.**
Don. 18/3-2/5/42.**H.**
Cow. 4-15/1/43.**L.**
Cow. 24/4-4/6/43.**L.**
Don. 28/1/44. *for rebuilding.*

BOILER:
8934.

SHEDS:
Haymarket.
Aberdeen 16/11/36.
Haymarket 23/10/42.

Withdrawn and Rebuilt to Class A2/2.

For the continued history of these engines readers are referred to Volume 3 in this series.

(above) **An order for the second locomotive was reinstated on 7th November 1933 to be numbered 2002, and Doncaster's register of New Engine Orders shows 5 altered to 1. This is how it appeared when ex works 6th October 1934, and it differed from its predecessor by having piston valves operated by the normal Walschaerts-Gresley valve gear, and no feed water heater was fitted, but at first it had the same arrangement of deflectors at the front.**

(below) Exactly a year after the previous order had been cut from 5 to only 1, another order for four was placed with Doncaster, and allocated engine numbers 2003 to 2006. Before 2003 was completed, experience with A4 class had shown that its streamlined front end gave the fully effective answer to smoke and steam clearance, so was applied to the four engines of that P2 order. Note however, that on them, the side valancing only extended to the rear of the cylinders. *British Railways.*

The piston valves gave very different exhaust steam characteristics from the poppet valves, and it was soon found that the single deflector plates did not clear the smoke and steam satisfactorily. Ex works 17th April 1935 additional plates had been fitted 17" away at their base, but only 6" at their top edge. The original plates had their leading edge cut back 12", and the beading on them was discarded; those alterations were sufficient to solve 2002's clearance problem.

With the first three all significantly different, it might have been expected that 2004 would be identical to 2003, and although substantially so, it was the only one of the six to be fitted with a by-pass valve to divert part of the exhaust steam away from the blastpipe. The valve control rod can be seen behind, and just above the front end of the vacuum ejector exhaust pipe.

2005 followed suit in being definitely different, and was the only one not to be fitted with double blastpipe and chimney, but the difference was not readily apparent, although this view does enable it to be recognised. 2005 retained its single exhaust arrangement throughout its existence as a P2, and that may have influenced its choice as the first to be changed to a Thompson Pacific.

The last of the class 2006 was completed on 5th September 1936, and differed from the previous five in having a longer firebox combustion chamber. That could be identified in views of either side because the extra length permitted five, instead of only four, access hand holes to be provided on the firebox.

The smoke clearing by the wedge-shaped front end was so successful that 2002 was changed to it at its first general repair from which it was ex works on 14th October 1936. No.2001 also got A4 type front end when from 30th September 1937 to 14th April it was also changed from poppet to piston valves, and the feed water heater was taken off. At least all six then looked as if they were brothers despite one being MONS MEG.

2004's by-pass valve proved troublesome; a butterfly valve at first, with its rod pulled to open it, and pushed to close it, carbonised oil caused it to stick. In July 1937 the valve was changed to plug type, now opened by pushing and closed by pulling the rod. As might have been expected, drivers tended to ignore it, so in June 1939 the manual control was replaced by automatic, working off the reversing shaft by linkage, which opened the plug valve when cut-off was 38% or longer.

The rubber sheet linking the cab roof with the tender caused complaints of hot conditions in the cab, so when 2006 was new, two extra sliding ventilators were provided, one above each seat. Note that its firebox had washing-out holes fitted with covers; the other five just had washout plugs.

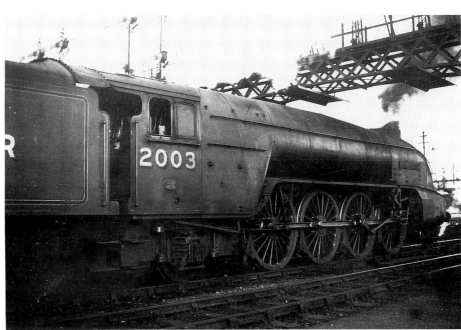

The cab on 2003 to 2006 was similar to that of the A4 class except the bottom edge was horizontal. The side sheets were straight, to match those of the tender, which had streamlined type front end, and neither had beading. The 4' 6" handrails were the same as had become standard on A4 class 4482, and subsequent engines.

During repairs in 1936 both 2001 and 2002 had their cab cut-out reduced in depth when backrests were added to the cab seats, and the handrails were also lengthened to 4' 3" between pillar centres. Note the tablet exchange apparatus fitted for working the short length of single line immediately south of Montrose, required by those running between Dundee and Aberdeen. Despite 2001 working mainly on the Edinburgh -Dundee section, it retained the full tablet exchange equipment. *R.K.Blencowe*

The tender with 2001 differed from the others in that its tank was welded, and its wheels were spoked. It remained coupled with 2001 throughout its life. 2002 got a standard high-sided non-corridor tender from a batch being built to run with new A3 class; those tenders had the usual riveted tanks and disc wheels.

From November 1941 all were changed from green to unlined black paint at their next repaint, and from July 1942 only N E appeared on the tender. 2004 was so treated when ex Cowlairs works on 26th February 1943 from a heavy repair as seen here near Stonehaven in June 1943. There are two other wartime changes of detail to be seen. The top lamp iron has been moved lower down so as to clear contact with the whistle when the smokebox door was lifted, and the streamlined casing in front of the cylinders has been partially removed.

2006 here on 1st April 1938 has just backed out of Doncaster works after repair, and was the first P2 to show that classification on the front buffer beam. Class parts were not included, 2006 being Part 3 because of its different firebox, the others being Part 2, Part 1 having disappeared with the streamlining of 2001 and 2002. This view also shows the drive from the rear coupled wheel for the Teloc speedometer with which all six were fitted.

When new, 2001 made a brief visit to Scotland for Gresley to show it to the Lord Provosts of Aberdeen and of Edinburgh, and there was public viewing in Waverley station. However, until the end of July it did not take up its allocation to the Haymarket shed in Edinburgh. So many new features were included that full trial of them was desirable, with ready access to works for any alterations. In mid-June it worked daily out of King's Cross on the 10.50 a.m. calling at all stations to Peterborough. It returned on the 2.48 p.m. express from Peterborough due in King's Cross at 4.15, which at York collected a portion from Scarborough, coaches from Hull at Doncaster, and at Peterborough some from Grimsby were added.

Following that mid-June week devoted to 'running-in', it then moved to work out of Doncaster shed and a couple of weeks were spent working trains with the dynamometer car included. They were the 11.04 a.m. from Doncaster, returning from London on the 4.00 p.m. which loaded to about 580 tons to Peterborough, and 420 tons thence to Doncaster. During those runs indicator diagrams were taken from the cylinders. Further runs on the same trains, but without the dynamometer car, were made in the next two weeks to check smokebox vacuum with differing diameters of blastpipe top, and the Kylchap cowls. COCK O' THE NORTH was then deemed to go live up to its name.

Here passing through Edinburgh's Princes Street Gardens, 2001 is on the work for which it was intended. It was first used regularly to take the 2.00 p.m. from Edinburgh to Dundee, and return from there with the 5.40 p.m.

Gresley's co-operation with the French expert Andre Chapelon led to arrangements being made for 2001 to be put through a series of tests at Vitry, and here on 4th December 1934 it is leaving Doncaster to go on the night ferry from Harwich to Calais. After the tests, and being put on display in Paris (Nord) station, it left France on 20th February 1935, and returned via the same route. *L.N.E.R.*

To evaluate what was learned from the tests, in April/May 1935, no.2001 again worked from Doncaster shed on their most exacting trains to and from King's Cross. The one which left there at 11.04 a.m. had portions from Halifax, Bradford, Ripon, Harrogate, and Hull added to the main train from Leeds, whilst the return at 4.00 from King's Cross loaded to almost 600 tons as already described.

2001 here at Inverkeithing in the summer of 1936 has again taken up its regular twice-daily express train trips to and from Dundee, and this view is typical of the curvature which inevitably punished an engine with such a long fixed wheelbase.

(left) Through running by the P2's between Edinburgh and Aberdeen was resumed during the war, and here 2001 on 21st September 1942 is at Montrose. Note that the casing in front of the cylinders has already been removed. From early 1939, the pair allocated to Haymarket shed were also used from Edinburgh to Glasgow (Queen Street) and back twice each day.

(below) After the fitting of its extra pair of smoke deflecting plates, 2002 also worked from Doncaster to and from King's Cross until returning with the 4 o'clock on 22nd May 1935, and after a check by the works, it then resumed its Dundee shed duties.

2002 was transferred from Dundee to Aberdeen shed in September 1936 and did the rest of its work based there. As seen here, one of its regular duties was the 7.35 p.m. sleeping car train to London - the 'Aberdonian' whose headboard it carries - which normally loaded to well over 500 tons, and on which it is at Ferryhill junction.

The passenger trains were not the only heavily loaded trains to be worked south from Aberdeen, and here in May 1938, with its rebuilt front end, 2002 is nearing Ferryhill junction with the 1.45 p.m. express fish and milk train to London and is well loaded.

The first of the four 1936 built engines no.2003 left the Doncaster paint shop on 13th June to be run in from Doncaster shed. Here it was caught at Newark working a Doncaster to Grantham all-stations train of only five vehicles, and it was seen at least once at King's Cross before it took up its Edinburgh Haymarket shed allocation on June 27th. *T.G.Hepburn.*

There is no doubt that 2004 made at least one visit to London whilst it was still cutting its teeth, and here they have given it the 600 ton 4 o'clock to haul to Doncaster, on 21st August 1936. This specific picture (but in full colour) was used for an officially issued jig-saw puzzle. *L.C.G.B. Ken Nunn coll.*

2005 was seen in London on 16th August 1936 before arriving at its home shed of Dundee on the 20th to share their duties with 2003. One was the 8.40 a.m. to Edinburgh, 2.00 p.m. Edinburgh to Aberdeen, and home on the 7.35 p.m. heavy sleeping car train. The kind of landscape it is crossing does not look as if it would be very lucrative for providing revenue for the railway.

2006 went into traffic on 5th September 1936, and whilst it only reached Scottish Area on the 23rd, it was not recorded as having worked to London in the interim. On 16th November 1936 it was transferred to Aberdeen shed from where it worked for the next six years, and here in August 1937 passing through Princes Street Gardens in Edinburgh, it is probably hauling the 5.35 p.m. to Aberdeen, because that was Ferryhill shed's only scheduled working out of Waverley. *W.Potter.*

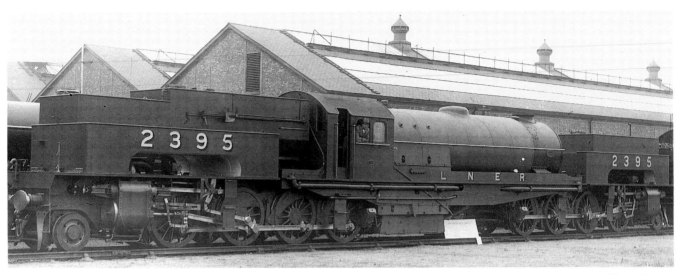

Before they sent it to run in the Stockton & Darlington Centenary procession, Doncaster made some changes and additions. A vent pipe was added to the front tank, lamp irons were put on above the buffer beams, and a vertical post was added at all four corners, to help access from steps on the front and below the buffer beam. Brackets to hold the fireirons were also fitted to the right hand side of the rear tank. The buffers were also changed to square flange and elliptical head, more in line with the type commonly used where the engine was going to do its work. After the procession, the engine was to be on static display at Darlington, where it would be viewed from ground level, and the L N E R initials on the tanks would not be seen. Both pairs were painted over, and replaced by a single set on the engine frame. The procession was on 1st July, and the static display was open to the public from the 4th to the 18th, and the engine then returned to Doncaster works for its running trials, after which they painted it the standard black, with single red lining (see pages 6 and 7). *L.N.E.R.*

This extra view of it whilst it was on display at Darlington is included to portray some details more clearly. Note the step on the front of the buffer beam, and the vertical rod and the step below it. Doncaster added one mounted on the main frame, behind the buffer beam and shown on the official photograph. The rodding seen on the right hand side of the firebox was for independent operation of the front and back dampers, and the ash pan had two hinged doors on each side. As the grate area was 54 sq. ft. provision had been made for rocking the front portion.

CLASS U1

2395

Beyer Peacock 6209.

To traffic 21/6/25.

REPAIRS:
Don. 26/7-25/8/26.**H.** *Re-tubed.*
Don. 14/7-8/10/27.**G.** *Firebox tubeplate cracked.*
Don. 25/9-9/2/29.**H.**
Don. 31/3/30. *To Plant for new firebox.*
Don. 20/10-11/12/30.**G.** *In shops for new firebox.*
Don. 1/3-10/5/32.**G.** *One new hornblock.*
Don. 26/2-2/5/34.**G.** *Ring control P.V.*
Don. 2/10-17/11/34.**H.** *Blowdown valve fitted.*
Don. 24/2-19/3/35.**L.**
Don. 10/9-12/10/35.**G.**
Don. 8/11/36-9/1/37.**G.**
Don. 17/10-17/11/37.**L.** *Tyres to turn.*
Don. 26/1-4/4/38.**G.**

Don. 17/7-15/8/38.**L.**
Don. 10/6-5/8/39.**G.**
Don. 18-30/9/39.**L.**
Don. 28/5-30/9/40.**G.** *New firebox.*
Don. 9-24/3/41.**L.** *Tank plates welded.*
Don. 15/8-19/9/42.**G.**
Don. 19/1-7/3/43.**L.** *L.H.cyl.fractured.*
Don. 21/3-8/5/43.**G.**
Don. 21/6-5/8/44.**G.**
Don. 23/3-1/6/45.**L.**
Don. 30/11/45-2/2/46.**L.**
Don. 5/8-2/11/46.**G.**
Don. 15/9-19/11/48.**G.**
Gor. 6/8/52-5/9/53.**L/I.**
Gor. 1/2/54-28/6/55.**N/C.**

BOILER:
7963.
Renumbered 27098 5/9/53.

SHEDS:
Gorton.
Doncaster 26/6/25.

Barnsley 21/8/25.
Mexborough 17/10/25.
LMRegion 7/3/49.
Mexborough 11/11/50.
Bromsgrove 3/7/55.
Burton 13/9/55.
Gorton 3/10/55.

RENUMBERED:
9999 17/3/46.
69999 19/11/48.

CONDEMNED:
23/12/55.
Cut up at Doncaster Works during February and March 1956.

The massive 7' 0" diameter boiler was fed by two no.12 Gresham & Craven injectors from a well between the frames in front of the firebox. Both tanks were connected to the well by a 5" diameter pipe just below the running plate on the right hand side, and with that through connection, the tanks could be filled from either end. Despite not being intended for any passenger work, it was originally fitted with couplings of the screw adjustable type, and it followed true Doncaster tradition by having two sets of guard irons on both ends, which it kept to withdrawal.

These were the rudimentary coaling facilities applicable to the Garratt when it was transferred in March 1949 to work assisting trains ascend the 1 in 37.7 of the Lickey incline, many of them passenger trains. Two of the more usual fare, in the shape of 0-6-0 Jinty 3F's, stand behind. The big engine was not amongst friends.

Both engine units were controlled by steam operated reversing gear located between the frame plates, and the operating rod for them is clearly seen below the running plate. Note the tall vent pipe which Doncaster added to the front tank, which was still to be seen until early in 1932. Although there was no difficulty with gauge clearance, it was then superseded by little more than a right angle bend.

The Garratt on a job entitling it to wear express passenger headlamp code? Yes indeed, and worthily, because it was carrying no less than the Lord Mayor of Sheffield. On 31st March 1930 it hauled a train of 20 special traffic wagons for display to Sheffield industrialists at Victoria station, an event put on by the Rotary Club, an international organisation I was invited, and glad, to join in 1941. The Sheffield Club's emblem was carried on the top lamp iron.

2395 was allocated to Mexborough for washing-out and maintenance, but was only to be seen there from Saturday afternoon until very early Sunday morning. This smoky atmosphere was common to all sheds late on Sundays, when the engines had their fires lit again, but real enthusiasts were quite untroubled about it. *L.N.E.R.*

War conditions also affected its owners' initials, because when ex works on 5th August 1944 they had been contracted from L N E R to only N E, as seen here later that month when it was drifting back down Worsborough bank to its refuge siding. On Sunday 17th March 1946, Mexborough shed changed 2395 to 9999 by stencilling, but Doncaster did change that to shaded transfers when sending it out on 2nd November 1946 although not troubling to restore L N E R to it. When they applied the British Railways 69999 numbering in November 1948, at its last general repair at that works, all five figures had tails so were not orthodox Gill Sans, but Gorton corrected that later. No smokebox number plate was ever fitted, a painted number on the buffer beam having to suffice, and that was missing when Gorton sent it out on 5th September 1953. *P.J.Hughes.*

When **69999** first went to Bromsgrove in March 1949 it began working chimney leading as it had invariably done on the LNER for more than 20 years. The LM Region crews found it difficult to judge distance to the rear of a train, so after three days its working position was reversed by turning it on a local triangle of lines. They were equally at a loss after dark, so by the end of March, it had acquired this car-type head lamp which was supplied from batteries in the box on the running plate. *L.Parker.*

The steam pipe supplying the engine at the cab end dropped down diagonally to pass beneath the firebox, and the ashpan was shaped to cater for it. That arrangement also helped to minimise heat loss in the necessarily long pipe. BRITISH RAILWAYS name and numbering had been applied when seen here alongside Bromsgrove coaling stage during the first of the two attempts to find useful work for it on the Lickey incline.

On the 10th March 1949 the Garratt backs up to the rear of a goods train at Bromsgrove three days after its arrival. Its mucky appearence leaves a lot to be desired and probably did not help in its initial acceptance by the Bromsgrove enginemen. An observer noted that the Bromsgrove men found the engine difficult to steam and, using their normal method of firing would see the fire going through the chimney. Another method of firing, backing the coal up under the firehole door, prevented the blast dispersing the fire but steam would drop dramatically by the time the top of the bank was reached. The brakes were apparently bad and some 200 yards were sometimes needed to bring the engine to a standstill. They found the "excessive power" would sometimes telescope vehicles at the rear of a train. It was obvious that the Midland men did not like the big engine and any and every excuse was used to get rid of it. A number of visits to Derby works made no difference, 69999 was not going to be accepted. *W.L.Good.*

When trains reached the top of the Lickey incline at Blackwell, 69999 dropped behind, then used the cross-over to coast down to Bromsgrove as here on 4th May 1949. It continued its work on the Lickey until November 1950 when it was returned to Mexborough where it was stored until the end of February 1951. It then did almost another year's work on Worsborough, before being stored again whilst its future was under consideration. The expense of a new boiler was ruled out, but money was found to convert it to firing by oil, and for that work it entered Gorton works on 6th August 1952, Doncaster works having done all its maintenance hitherto. *H.C.Casserley.*

In 1952 a change was made from coal to oil fuel, and a 5000 gallon oil tank was substituted for the bunker. Note its conspicuous filler, the two mushroom type air vents, and the different brackets for the changed fire irons. *The LNER Garratt Appreciation Society.*

The scene inside Gorton works during the conversion of the Garratt from coal to oil firing. The rear bunker has gone and the engine awaits its new oil tank. *William Lees per John Lees.*

During its second visit to Bromsgrove effective steps had been taken to nullify any excuses of misjudging distance due to inadequate lighting, because this powerful electric lamp had been fitted at the leading end, and it was powered by the turbogenerator which was part of the oil firing equipment. The electric lighting however was limited to only one end, and no advantage was taken of its availability to fit marker lights. *B.Hilton.*

The conversion to oil fuel lacked impetus, and various snags emerged so it was 11th October 1953 before it was able to run the trial seen here. To do so gave it one of the rare opportunities to actually haul a train, this being of 43 wagons and providing a load of about 600 tons, which it took from Dewsnap to Crowden and back. Further trial runs were made spasmodically until well into 1954, when it was again laid aside in store. *B.K.B.Green.*

For that lengthy period of storage, it was Gorton works which had to find space, as seen here on 13th March 1955, and where it stayed until on 29th June 1955. It was then again sent to Bromsgrove, where it proved no more welcome than before, so it was only at work until 13th September 1955 by when London Midland Region had found enough excuses to rid themselves of it. This time there was no further work for it on Worsborough, so withdrawal became inevitable. *J.F.Aylard.*

After LM Region had succeeded in getting rid of it, by treating it with what was almost 'dumb insolence' it was in store for almost two years, and by its official withdrawal on 23rd December 1955 it was already in Doncaster scrap yard, and this is how it was last photographed on 17th February 1956. By March 11th the only part that could be identified was three pairs of its driving wheels. *J.Wallbank.*